KARL BARTH AND THE PROBLEM OF WAR

KARL BARTH AND THE PROBLEM OF WAR

studies in christian ethics series

JOHN H. YODER

Nashville ABINGDON PRESS New York

KARL BARTH AND THE PROBLEM OF WAR

ISBN 0-687-20724-X

Library of Congress Catalog Card Number: 71-124760

SET UP, PRINTED, AND BOUND BY
THE PARTHENON PRESS, AT NASHVILLE,
TENNESSEE, UNITED STATES OF AMERICA

to the memory of one who faithfully filled
the office of teacher in the church

PREFACE

In 1954 I was asked by Jean Lasserre to present to Karl Barth his gift of a copy of *La Guerre et l'Evangile;* the gist of Lasserre's word of dedication in the flyleaf was "To Karl Barth, who taught me to rethink my faith in the light of the Word of God."

American Protestants, to whom the thought of Karl Barth was transmitted usually half a generation late and often through the filter of American controversies he did not mean to speak to, and then evaluated more as a philosophy than as proclamation, can hardly sense how simply fitting and how widely true is the statement that a generation of pastors were compelled by his work to rethink their faith, and to preach it, in the light of the overwhelming difference it makes if God has really spoken.

Only my sharing in this kind of esteem can explain the sustained attention to Barth's thought which underlies this attempt at rigorous yet respectful critique. A few other theologians have written about the issues of war and pacifism in such a way as to merit serious reading and response; there is hardly another whose thought has such rootedness and texture as to demand that the response be to his entire work. This study is then most properly understood if it is seen as a grateful tribute to the stature of a teacher who was above the need to want those who learned from him to become his disciples.

The study has benefited from comment and contributions of Clarence Bauman, Hannes de Graaf, Heinz Kloppenburg, Paul Ramsey, James Gustafson, and Roger Shinn. Its final rewriting was facilitated by the Institute of Mennonite Studies and the Schowalter Foundation.

JOHN H. YODER

CONTENTS

INTRODUCTION:
The Abiding Relevance of Our Topic

In the years since the nucleus of this text was first informally circulated, nothing has changed on either the political or the theological scene to diminish the relevance of the question with which it wrestles.

The Washington-Moscow diplomatic polarity, so self-evident in the mid-fifties, is no longer quite on the center of the world stage. Current Christian social thought is giving more of its attention to the "third world" and to the "theology of revolution." Yet the dimensions of the armed conflicts still going on during the period when the "cold war" was supposed to be "thawing," and the continuing nuclear threat, with more dangers of escalation and proliferation than there were ten years ago, make the moral challenge represented by war no less urgent for Christian thought in the 1970's than in the 1950's when Germany was nearer the center of the fear of world war.

Nor has there been any fundamental change within the churches or within theology to modify the urgency of the war question. The ecumenical movement has heightened the recognition, by most Christians, of the need for the church to rise above a narrow identification with one nation. Christian thinking about the mission of the church in the world is placing increasing emphasis upon the need to identify the moral responsibility of Christians within the structure of society. It is being said with increasing force in ecumenical meetings that Christians should "get out into the world"; but there is growing embarrassment when they ask just what they should and should not do there, for just what reasons and with what hopes.

Specific efforts to carry on conversation in an ecumenical context about matters closely related to this concern have been inconclusive. A common testimony entitled "Peace Is the Will of God," submitted to the World Council of Churches in 1953/54 by representatives of the historic peace churches and the International Fellowship of Reconciliation, could have no official status at the 1954 General Assembly; the only public response it received was from Angus Dun and Reinhold Niebuhr as individuals in *Christianity and Crisis,* June 13, 1955.

The WCC Department of Studies administered in 1955-57 a task force study dealing with "The Lordship of Christ over Church and World," which sought to lay the foundations for an ecumenical approach to the Christian political prophecy largely within the *heilsgeschichtlich* approach then current in ecumenical theology. The group's meetings were discontinued without an agreed result. During the same period another study group dealt with "Christians and the Prevention of War in an Atomic Age." Its report when received was emphatically designated as "A Provisional Study Document," and as "but a first step in a continuing study process"; yet the study process was not continued.[1] The concept of the "responsible society," after having been adopted at the Amsterdam Assembly of the World Council of Churches, was widely echoed between the Evanston Assembly in 1954 and the New Delhi Assembly in 1961, especially with reference to countries in the midst of rapid social change, but it has not been applied as intensively to the problems which social ethics faces in the West. The phrase has since 1948 found wide acceptance as a motto, but there is increasing question among ethicists as to how much more it is than just a motto. The primary institutional vehicle for the propagation of the concept "responsible society" from Amsterdam

[1] The document was later published under the names of the Commission's officers: Robert Billheimer and T. M. Taylor, *Christians and the Prevention of War in an Atomic Age* (London: SCM Press, 1961).

1948 through Delhi 1961 was a series of studies on the responsibility of the church in areas of rapid social change. This gave to some the impression that the slogan had been coined for use by the "younger churches" in the "new nations." Yet the Amsterdam documents make clear that this was not the issue when the phrase was born; then the concern was to find a middle way between socialism and free-enterprise visions of the society Christians should want in the West. This Western character of the way the slogan "responsible society" sets up the questions has since been increasingly perceived, and the phrase has largely dropped out of currency since the Geneva Church and Society conference of 1966. In any case, its application is primarily to the problems which arise *within* a given social order. For the problem of war, it is the least likely to be of help.

In the past decade ethical theory has seen a renewal of concern for the language of the traditional theory of "just war," with a few Protestant thinkers—most notably Paul Ramsey—and some Catholic ones strongly committed to the renewal of the kind of disciplined moral responsibility for the evaluation of any given war which that tradition represents. On the other hand the same period has seen a renewed advocacy of a radical ethical relativism under the label of "contextualism." Neither thrust has swept the field, and neither has found new words to speak convincingly on modern war. The decade has seen an abundance of "new beginnings" which promised to change the shape of our discussion, but without evident fruit thus far. The slogan "new morality" has reached wide currency thanks to the journalistic-programmatic writings of J. A. T. Robinson, who gave this title to a chapter of his best seller, *Honest to God*. Its most visible casuistic implementation has been volunteered by Joseph Fletcher and James A. Pike, claiming elements of support in the systematic writings of Paul Lehmann as well as Bultmann, Bonhoeffer, Brunner, and Barth, though not all of them would agree to Fletcher's claim that they support him.

The quality of serious ethical discourse which the present monograph advocates, and to which the series in which it takes its place is dedicated, is not what these popularizers are attacking, and no attempt is to be made here to respond to them. They are not so much wrong (and certainly they are not so new) as they are careless, contradictory, and without fruit in terms of disciplined moral guidance.[2] The "death of God" theologians said they would point us to the "contagious" radicality of Jesus, as the substitute for a no longer believable divine transcendence, but the fad died before anyone could spell out what that would mean for political ethics. The more recent call for a "theology of revolution" simply repeats the logic of the classical "just war" tradition with the roles reversed and with "hope" its watchword. If we ask with any care why men should focus their hope in revolution, and in what kind of revolution, we find that the changing of the words has brought us not one step forward.

The need for a new Christian appraisal of the problem of war is evident to everyone. Few in our time would defend with conviction the traditional positions used by Christian theologians to justify the participation of Christians in war, as if they needed no review in the face of the new weaponry.

The chief result of past debate between pacifism and its critics has been to make clear that none of the traditional positions in the field of discussion has demonstrated a solution to the problems caused by war and especially by modern war. At the same time these discussions have shown clearly the absolute urgency of finding an answer to this problem above all others.

As the result of the last half-century of history and theology there remain only two positions really in the field, only two considered and worked-out ways of looking at the problem of war.[3] On the one hand there is the view which is sometimes called "chastened pacifism," i.e., a kind of thinking which differs from what one might call the "classical humanistic" pacifism of the thirties in its full awareness of the problems of sin and of the state. On the other hand there is "chastened non-pacifism,"

[2] J. A. T. Robinson, *Honest to God* (London: SCM Press, 1963). Joseph Fletcher, *Situation Ethics* (Philadelphia: Westminster Press, 1966). James A. Pike, *You and the New Morality* (New York: Harper, 1967). Paul Lehmann, *Ethics in a Christian Context* (New York: Harper, 1963). Cf. Paul Ramsey's critique in *Deeds and Rules* (New York: Scribner's, 1967) and James M. Gustafson, "Context *versus* Principles: A Misplaced Debate in Christian Ethics" in *Harvard Theological Review,* LVIII (1965), 171 ff.

[3] To say of any question that there are but two positions in the field is evidently a sweeping simplification. Most positions held in the past are still held by someone in the present. Such a statement is true only in the small universe of discourse for which it is primarily written, that is, for positions being actively represented within the mainstream of ecumenical Protestant social thought as carried by those schools, journals, and publishers which have a constituency beyond the historic denominations. The limiting terms in the above sentence are "considered" and "worked-out."

the position of those Christian thinkers who, although they advocate, at least as a possibility, an eventual Christian participation in war, concede an element of truth in Christian pacifism. Karl Barth speaks for this latter posture.

Thus the continuing conversation on Christian moral responsibility in a world at war may still be served by a careful encounter with the most monumental body of theologically integrated Protestant ethical thought which our century has seen. Even those who disagree with Barth's theology will gain from an encounter with his erudition, vision, and consistency of method. The reader with no prior loyalty to a given school of thought may find his own meditation about the nature of ethics and about the problem of war tested and clarified by the exercise of thinking things through in Barth's terms.

This study seeks to interpret briefly the corpus of Karl Barth's writings on war, which, as we shall see, represents an innovation unparalleled in mainstream Protestant theology. I shall not attempt to footnote literally every assertion made about Barth's views, partly because the purpose of this study is not to achieve the degree of thoroughness expected of doctoral dissertations, and partly because his works, written over a long period of time, do not always make entirely clear, in so many words and without paraphrase, especially to the American reader, everything that is necessary to understand fully his position.

This exposition, written with the intention of conveying a grasp of Barth's approach as a whole, may even seem to contradict the apparent sense of certain passages in Barth's writings. I am conscious of this possibility; my own understanding of Barth's way of looking at Christian ethics thought is based, in part, on personal conversations. I wish here to express my deep gratitude for the privilege of having discussed with Professor Barth, both before and after drafting this study, certain questions not fully dealt with in his written works.[4]

[4] Since the body of this text is a running exposition of a limited number of Barth's writings, the source references are provided in parentheses within the text. The footnotes are not source references but byways of thought, significant in their own substance but not immediately in the line of the argument. *KD* refers to the German original of the doctrinal magnum opus, *Kirchliche Dogmatik* (Zollikon-Zürich: Evangelischer Verlag, 1932-1967); *CD* to its English translation, *Church Dogmatics,* eds. G. W. Bromiley and T. F. Torrance (Edinburgh: T. and T. Clark, 1936-1962).

I

The Mode and Manners of Theological Ethics

The earlier drafts of this text were prepared at Basel in the course of my doctoral studies in the faculty of theology. A text substantially similar to the present one was read by Professor Barth in the summer of 1957. After a conversation following that reading, a number of points in the original text were changed to guard against misunderstanding. Such clarifications have been incorporated into the present text. However, at no point did the paper's argument rest upon a mistaken understanding of Professor Barth's position and intention.

On the other hand, the conversation with Professor Barth made it seem useful to precede the present text by a few remarks concerning the nature, intent, and etiquette of theological ethics. This is all the more desirable because the present study, over and above the specific controversy on the subject of war, may be viewed as well as a sample exercise seeking to throw light on the larger question, "How should Christians think about ethics?" These remarks are of a general character; they do not belong particularly to a discussion of Karl Barth and pacifism any more than they would to a treatment of Thomas Aquinas and celibacy or of Calvin and usury; yet the peculiar shape of our problem, its present political relevance, and the etiquette problems of contemporary American ethical debate, make them more necessary at this point.

1. Theological ethics is, like all other human discourse, limited in its validity. To be absolutely precise, every statement should be formulated in the conditional mode, and every criticism in the form of a question. "If I understand correctly it would seem that . . ." would strictly speaking be the proper way to begin every sentence. We generally omit the formula because we agree that it is always understood. What is true in general of theological ethics is true even more of this paper, since we are obliged, especially toward the end, to extrapolate Barth's position at points where he did not express himself systematically.

2. Ethics, like the rest of Christian theology, has Christian revelation as its norm and is a careful intellectual (Barth would say "scientific") discipline. It therefore deals with arguments, measuring their conformity to the norm of revelation, without passing judgment on the moral or other qualities of those who present the arguments. Barth expresses this fact in his distinction between ethos and ethics (cf. below, p. 24). Ethos is how we actually behave; ethics is how we responsibly think about our behavior. Ethics as a theological discipline should deal with arguments cold-bloodedly, critically, and without respect to persons. The measure of the brotherly character of Christian ethical polemics will not be its mildness, but its clarity, accuracy, and objectivity of the appeal to the criterion of revelation. The reader who might feel that the present study is too uninhibited in the questions it addresses to Barth is advised to compare its tone with that of Barth's own criticisms of Emil Brunner or Lorraine Boettner.

That a criticism of Barth's arguments does not involve a criticism of his person should theoretically not need to be said; two considerations however make it necessary:

a. There are critics of Barth who attack him from quite another quarter and who, intentionally or not, give the impression that his views on war and rearmament have nothing to do with his theology; consequently such criticism of Barth often amounts to calling into question his intelligence or his personal integrity.[1] I do not intend to carry on the discussion on such a level.

b. By the nature of the case, we are driven to deal (below, pp. 82 ff.) with Barth's choice to support Switzerland's military preparedness during World War II. Here of course the danger of confounding argument and arguer in the same criticism is still greater; but also here I intend to deal solely with the arguments, respecting for the purposes of my discussion with Barth the distinction which he himself made between ethos and ethics, even though the line becomes hard to draw. Of interest in Barth's attitude during the war years is not so much what he decided and did, but whether the reasons he gave for his decisions and actions, which happen to be our main source of information on his understanding of the state, are convincing theologically.

3. Barth's position is in many ways very near that of Christian pacifism (cf. pp. 38, 51 and 81 below), nearer in fact than that of any really prominent theologian in the history of European Protestant dogmatics. The area of disagreement discussed in the critical second part is thus in fact far narrower than the area in which Barth agrees with Christian pacifists, as we together criticize the more traditional Protestant theologies of the past and the present. This situation raises two questions:

a. The question of principle. Is it appropriate to concentrate upon a point which is not the center of the gospel for Barth (nor for the pacifist either, if he is a Christian), and to devote this amount of attention to the illumination and evaluation of a disagreement at just this one point? Is it fair, with the thoroughness I have here sought to achieve, to put the question, "How can Barth justify war?" when Barth's main point is that war is almost never justifiable?

b. The question of expediency. Is it opportune to carry on a discussion of this question between these very nearly agreed positions when the advocates of both have their hands full debating with their common theological adversaries, and struggling with the common task of averting World War III?

It is healthy to raise these questions. They remind us of the modest

[1] This was most strikingly the case for the first American reactions to brief press reports of Barth's 1958 "Letter to a Pastor in the German Democratic Republic" (first full American trans. in R. M. Brown, ed., *How to Serve God in a Marxist Land* [New York: Association Press, 1959], pp. 45 ff.

scope of the discussion we are carrying on, and remind us that the discussion proceeds in a context dominated by far-reaching agreement. They do not, however, lead us to conclude that further discussion should be abandoned.

4. Barth himself began the conversation with his treatment of pacifism in his *Church Dogmatics,* Vol. III/4. He did so in a way which to most pacifists seems to show an inadequate understanding of their position. He did not hesitate to make use of his polemic talents, and, although the accuracy of his understanding of his interlocutors can be questioned, he addressed himself to them by name on a platform to which they have no access. To leave the matter there would be in contradiction to Barth's own views as to the "conversational" character of theology, and would still not keep the question of Christian participation in war from being discussed on a less serious plane and in a way less worthy of theological attention.

5. Not only Barth's theological adversaries but also many who consider themselves his disciples have misunderstood what he meant with his crucial, not easily translated concept of *Grenzfall* (the extreme case in which killing may be willed by God), and have thereby exaggerated his willingness to conceive of war as an acceptable choice. Not only the expository first section of this book, but also that part of the second section which deals critically with the *Grenzfall* (pp. 64 ff.) attempt to clarify the extent of Barth's agreement with pacifists, and to defend his intention against the overzealous interpretations of some "Barthians."

6. It is of the nature of theology that the nearer two positions are, the more necessary and the more serious the conversation between them becomes. Barth himself is much less sharp in his criticism of Roman Catholic theologians or of Schleiermacher than in that of his Protestant colleagues. The greater the context of agreement, the greater is the importance of coming to grips with remaining disagreements, in order to ascertain whether they are truly superficial or whether they conceal much deeper differences. Further conversation with Barth's position may well lead to the discovery that he was not so far from pacifism as he thought and said (a possibility which I am not willing to exclude, despite the difficulties experienced in carrying on an exchange of views). Or if further discussion had led him to define more explicitly his disagreement with pacifists, we might have discovered that he was not so far from the

traditional Protestant view as he had seemed. In either case such conversation would have been worthwhile.

The Problem of Approach

In addition to his monumental systematic writings, Karl Barth was politically active far more than most of his professional colleagues. As a churchman and as a concerned citizen he spoke to political issues from the Christian perspective, most often with special regard to the problems of the state, police, and totalitarianism.

In a briefer pamphlet I have treated the occasional and the systematic writings as two separate bodies of literature, following each independently until, by somewhat different itineraries, they came out at about the same place in explaining the position of Barth the churchman.[2] Here, however, we shall follow the sequence of argument of the *Church Dogmatics,* since our concern is less with immediate political involvement than with the structure of Barth's thought. We shall fall back upon the occasional documents only after an initial outline, especially where they might throw light on issues not dealt with in the *Dogmatics.*

Both for Barth and for Christian pacifists, the question of pacifism is not the central question of the Christian faith. Rather, it is only one of the chapters within the discipline of Christian ethics, which in turn is but one of the chapters within the far greater theological repertory. Accordingly, in this exposition of Barth's views we must discuss much more than just what he has to say about war. Indeed, we must discuss more than just what he has to say about ethics. This is especially necessary because, perhaps more than any other thinker in recent times, Barth approaches every question "systematically," i.e., with exactly the same orientation: he seeks to relate everything to the same center. To understand his thinking on any one question, then, we must consider not only that question itself, but also the way in which Barth proceeds from the center of Christian faith, i.e., from the revealing, reconciling, and redeeming work of God in Christ, to deal with the particular issue.

After discussing Barth's approach, I shall attempt to sketch those points

[2] John Yoder, "The Pacifism of Karl Barth," Church Peace Mission pamphlet No. 5, trans. from the French by the author (Scottdale, Pa.; Herald Press, 1964).

of difference which have become visible and which must be the object of further conversation between Barth's position and that of Christian pacifists. Rather than make a positive case for pacifism, I shall only indicate those points at which Barth's argument will be least convincing to Christian pacifists.

II

The Nature and Claim of the Discipline of Christian Ethics

A short summary of the argument of the *Church Dogmatics,* Vol. II/2, where the place of ethical deliberation within the rest of theology is dealt with, must precede the conclusions drawn concerning the method of ethical thought.[1]

The theological science of Christian ethics, according to Barth, does not contribute directly to moral decision, nor does it evaluate the ultimate righteousness (before God) of decisions which have been made. It has a much more modest function. Its only task is to test, technically and "scientifically," i.e., carefully, with relation to the object of Christian faith, the reasons Christians give to account for their actions before, in the course of, or after having made their decisions. The science of Christian dogmatics, or "systematic theology," to use the more current American

[1] Since I am largely following the sequence of the original text, specific source references will seldom be needed. The translation is that of *CD* unless indicated as directly from *KD.*

term, is not itself a part of preaching but only a critique of the way in which preaching is done and a testing of preaching in the light of the norm of faith which is God's self-revelation in Christ. Likewise ethics is not the making of decisions but simply the critique and testing, with the criteria provided by God in his revelation, of the arguments, reasons, and explanations given by Christians to describe their deciding. Thus in Christian action, just as in Christian thinking, we must begin by admitting the priority of God's speaking over our speaking about God. In Christian moral decision, just as in Christian preaching, the basic event is the Word of God, and that Word is not in human hands. Man can no more capture the Word of God with an ethical discussion about the process of decision than he can capture the Word of God with a doctrinal discussion about the contents of Christian preaching. The discipline of *ethics* must therefore be distinguished from the field of *ethos,* that area where decision, action, and responsibility take place before God, in the encounter with his command. The field of ethos is where what really matters happens. Ethics, the discipline in which we discuss the reason for decision and action, is at best only a handservant to Christian ethos.

The final section of *CD* II/2 is most directly relevant to our later concerns. Under the heading "The Command as the Decision of God," Barth is preoccupied with the difference between an ethic rooted in the Word of God and the way philosophical ethics normally proceeds. The correlate terms *sovereignty* and *responsibility* demonstrate how man is taken from the pose of making his own decisions and placed instead in a context of accountability before God.

The divine decision is not only sovereign but *definite;* it does not promulgate generalities which we then on our own figure out how to apply in concrete cases: it speaks specifically in concrete cases, as God's Word always enters into the limits of space and time. The divine decision is *good:* it is not simply an enunciation of goodness already discerned elsewhere but rather the definition of goodness in the commanding of it.

This amounts to a rejection not only of most philosophical ethics but of many efforts to carry on theological ethics after a similar model: reasoning from general statements (assumed to be the more clear and divine the more they are general) to specifics (increasingly less sure as they get closer to cases). Barth analyzes carefully some biblical commandments, including those where the literal statement appears to be quite general, like the Decalogue, to support his claim for the definiteness of the command in every situation to which God speaks.

It is then of course necessary for Barth to come to grips with the fact that there seems to be, in the Old and the New Testaments as well as in Christian history, considerable casuistic teaching, i.e. application of general rules to specific cases. The Decalogue in the Old Testament and the Sermon on the Mount in the New are cast sweepingly in the form of commandments or prohibitions concerning what we should or should not do in certain cases. Barth replies that ethical teachings, such as the commands which are preserved for us in the Sermon on the Mount or in the Decalogue, are not given with the intention that they be understood as general principles from which deduction for specific cases would be possible, but rather as samples or specimens, as "indications" of the general direction which God's commandment usually follows. They are indications of the form which Christian ethos will usually take, but they are not standards of value which can reliably, in the hands of men alone, be applied to every decision with the certainty that in every place at every time it would thereby be possible to choose the right act.

Then the question arises: Is there such a thing as Christian ethics at all? If it is not possible to state valid general principles, and if even those parts of Scripture which are stated in the form of specific commandments cannot be taken as universally valid orders which apply automatically and obviously to Christian obedience in every relevant case, then the question is not only possible but inevitable: In what sense is it possible to speak at all about Christian obedience? In what sense are we capable of saying anything which would not be an offense against the sovereignty of God, an attempt to tie God down? Barth responds that to hide behind such a question would be going too far. Christian ethics is possible, first, because the Word of God includes his commandments and because the Word which God speaks to every time and place is always Jesus Christ. Though he will speak this Word to every time and at every place with a new immediacy and relevance, in a new relationship to every new situation, the Word remains the same Word which he has spoken to men in Christ. There is thus a very considerable portion of parallel content and of coincidence among all the commandments, which permits us, not to draw casuistic conclusions from generalities, but still, with a real degree of helpfulness, to discern major emphases within the words and commands which God has spoken in the past in Christ himself and through the apostles and prophets.

Second, Barth would say that Christian ethics is possible because, despite the limits of our knowledge, we can say *some* things about the situation to which God speaks. We can never know and define fully or adequately the human situation; every ethical choice takes place in a new situation which is, even for the agent himself, and especially for an observer, not completely knowable. Yet there are constants in man's nature, in human creatureliness, which make it possible for us to say something meaningful and valid about the locus where God's Word strikes men.

This prefatory discussion provides the necessary context for what we will have to say later about more concrete problems, such as those connected with the taking of human life. We had to remind ourselves of what Barth intends to do in Christian ethics. In order neither to overestimate nor underestimate affirmations and denials, we must keep in mind that it is not Barth's intention to ask, either about the past or about the present, whether a decision made in faith is in God's eyes the right one or not. A decision made for the wrong conscious reasons may yet by the grace of God be the right decision. Barth's only interest is to measure, in confrontation with the yardstick of God's revelation, the explanations which the Christian can bring forward to interpret his decision to himself and to his brothers.

III
Reverence for Life

We turn now to examine the outline of Barth's exposition of Christian ethics as we find it in the third volume of his great work. Ethics in *Church Dogmatics III* is ethics within the framework of creation. Barth does not yet speak of ethics within the framework of reconciliation nor of ethics within the framework of redemption; those themes are reserved for later. Here his concern is for what it means for ethics that man is *creature.*

In earlier parts of the work Barth identifies four characteristics which serve as his definition of man as creature; in Volume III/4 he develops ethics along these four lines. First, man is man in that he is free before God for fellowship with God. Second, man is man in that he exists in togetherness with other human creatures: with woman, with his neighbor, with the community, with the nation. Third, man is man in that he is alive. He is the soul of his body. Fourth, it is constitutive of man to be limited. Within each of these four dimensions of humanity Barth proceeds to discuss certain questions of ethics.

The section with which we shall have to deal is the third of these, that which deals with man as a life, as alive (*CD* III/4, 324-564). We will view the question of war within the framework of the larger question concerning the meaning of life, the value of life as a creation of God, and the ways in which that value is limited. We must go into a certain degree of detail before approaching the question of war, for Barth's reasoning on different sides of the question moves in parallels. What he says about various ways of taking life and various kinds of respect for life is useful for understanding what he means when he writes about war.

Without intending to include in the term all that Albert Schweitzer meant by it, Barth takes up the slogan which Schweitzer had chosen as the core of his ethical thinking, "Reverence for Life." The physical life of man is "a good" (*ein Gut*) because it is the presupposition for his obedience. It is as a living creature that man is called upon to obey God. But having said that life is "a good," we must also say that it is but a relative good. Its value is limited by the value of obedience itself. If obedience should call for the surrender of life, then we could no longer hide behind the statement that life is good: that would be to refuse obedience (*CD* 334-35).

Within this framework Barth deals first with the values of animal life, e.g., instinct, health, joy, and power, before proceeding to the section "The Protection of Life." Since life is only a proximate value, its protection, that is, the protection of the good which in the will of the creating God is dependent upon life, can require its abandonment. Such a paradox is not within man's power for calculation; it is not up to man to decide when he has reached the point at which, instead of preserving life, he is called to take or to sacrifice life. That extreme limit can be reached only when God so commands. But then the defense of life can under certain conditions, when the commanding God will have it so, also involve the destruction and breaking down of life. "Then and only then, but then with all seriousness, when God as the Lord of life just this time will have it this way and not otherwise" (*CD* III/4, 398; here translated more literally from *KD* III/4, 454). It is thus a possibility, within the freedom of God—since God is Lord of life, and since life is good only as a vehicle for obedience to him—to say, in such an exceptional case, that the protection of life consists in the taking of life.

From such an understanding arises the difference between killing and murder. Killing, the taking of life in exceptional cases when God would have it so, is an expression of the respect for life, whereas murder is the taking of life which man permits himself when he ascribes to himself sovereignty over life and when he himself decides when life is to be abandoned. The Ten Commandments exclude murder. At the same time it is clear that the legislation of ancient Israel did by no means intend to exclude legitimate killing. The same is the case in Matthew 5 and I John 3, in passages which radically sharpen the intensity of the prohibition of *murder,* but which do not go so far as to prohibit all *killing.* Barth argues that the apostle Peter himself, with his words, literally killed Ananias and Sapphira (Acts 5). He picks up as well the statement of Paul in I Corinthians 5, according to which church discipline can or should have the result of "destroying the flesh." Likewise, all the New Testament makes it clear that the legitimate bearer of the authority of the state may kill. That is affirmed not only in the classical passage of Romans 13:1-7, but also, and perhaps with a greater degree of theological depth, in John 19:11 (Jesus' word to Pilate), "You would have no power over me unless it had been given you from above."

It is indeed a matter for surprise, Barth remarks (*CD* 400), that, after the incarnation in which human life was taken up by God himself in Christ, after the crucifixion where human death was likewise assumed and absorbed by Christ, and after the resurrection when death's power was broken, the New Testament does not simply declare all killing to be out of the question. It is clear that the New Testament reckons much less than the Old Testament with the possibility of cases where killing is necessary; the improbability and infrequency of such cases in the New Testament clearly calls us to vigilance and to hesitancy before we may conclude that we have come to the point where the taking of life is commanded. Yet the New Testament clearly does not forbid killing. "On the basis of the incarnation and crucifixion the protection of life has received the sharpness and intensity which obliges us to push further and further back the border between killing which may be commanded as *ultima ratio* and murder which is forbidden" (*KD* 456). This pushing back of the border between legitimate and illegitimate killing is undeniably the burden of the New Testament; yet it still has not been pushed back infinitely. There is still room beyond it for killing.

Subsequently the two concepts of "murder" and "killing" serve as fixed categories to frame the question whether the taking of a given life is wrong. Before speaking of the problem of war, Barth treats a series of other problems in the protection of life: suicide, abortion, euthanasia, self-defense, and the death penalty. On each of these points he first says very clearly, in line with the foundation already laid, that the taking of life is not right. The protection of life is the command of God, and the command of God applies to all these fields. Yet at almost every point he feels obliged to qualify the statement by leaving room for the extreme case where the taking of life can still be commanded by God. Since this is very closely related to the line of reasoning which he later applies to war, it is instructive to see how the procedure functions in these other fields.

In the instance of suicide, Barth begins the transition from command to exception with the parenthetical remark that suicide is not necessarily worse or less forgivable than any other kind of killing. A person who kills himself is not any further from the forgiveness of God, because of the fact that he no longer lives to repent, than a person who would have wrongly killed someone else. The judgment of God, which the suicide like any other sinner must encounter, is a judgment of grace. Judas in the New Testament and Saul in the Old are symbolic of what the Word of God thinks of suicide; what is condemned by Scripture in Saul and in Judas is not so much the taking of life as the pride, the revolt against the election of God, the self-sovereignty which he who kills himself usurps. The fact that Judas and Saul are roundly condemned by Scripture is not so much a condemnation of the act of killing oneself as it is a condemnation of the spiritual attitude of one who takes it into his own hands to undo the work of grace, especially the grace of his own calling.

At the beginning of his discussion of the protection of life, Barth states on what might be called systematic grounds that the protection of life can sometimes consist in its sacrifice; now he must raise the question: Can it ever be that the protection of life, which as a general rule means that suicide is forbidden, may in certain cases mean the contrary? Can it ever be that the protection of the purpose of life can demand suicide?

Barth raises several hypothetical possibilities which leave it open that such could be the case. The dilemma of a person, who, if remaining alive, is in danger of being forced to betray secrets that would endanger the lives of others might be an example of this possibility. The man who stands before a concrete choice, however, cannot simply affirm, on the basis of the belief that other lives are in danger, or of a similar calculation, that now the time has come when he must kill himself. Barth is much more careful.

> The possibility of the extreme case, here as elsewhere, is a particular possibility belonging to God himself; it is permitted to no one simply to persuade himself that this extreme case has come for him. That can only be commanded to a man. If he kills himself without having received the command to do so, then his act is murder. (*KD* 470; cf. *CD* 413.)

With thoroughness and consistency Barth seeks to eschew all casuistics. He tries not to affirm that suicide is in general wrong, but that in certain specified kinds of cases it is right.[1] The rightness of suicide is something which can never be affirmed by men; it can only be commanded by God. Even if a man is sure in his own calculations and in his own understanding of the situation that there is no other way, precisely that certainty is no justification for his making an exception to the commandment of God that life be respected. Only the command of God himself can render that exception real.

At this point the critical reader might well ask: "How then will one know that suicide is now commanded?" If this "can only be commanded" (more literally, "this is something which must be *said* to a man"), how is this "saying" of God to be perceived? We shall return to this question at length later. It relates to Barth's entire conception of the Word of God. That he does not provide a clear answer here (or at the other points where the reference to the commanded exceptional case would raise it) is not an evasion but a part of his point. To answer it would be to fall back into the confident casuistics which he seeks to avoid.

Next Barth faces the problem of abortion (*CD* 415 ff.). Again it is

[1] Here Barth differs from the "new moralists" who in order to undercut an old casuistic must establish a countercasuistic and demonstrate in advance for certain hypothetical cases that the action forbidden by the old casuistic would be right after all.

clear that the will of God is the preservation of life. Again it is clear that man has no right to make exceptions. Again there can be the extreme case in which it can be the will of God for the life of an embryo to be sacrificed intentionally. Contrary to his general procedure elsewhere, Barth enumerates certain conditions (*CD* 421 ff.); these conditions, however, are not to be understood in a casuistic sense, but rather as attempts to make still more clear how extreme the case must be for it ever to be possible to say that God commanded the killing. For example, the first condition is that it must be a matter of life against life. Abortion for the sake of convenience, for the avoidance of psychological shock, to avoid illegitimate birth even as the result of rape, for economic reasons, or for reasons of health cannot be justified. Only if it is clear that a developing pregnancy really threatens the life of a mother can it be permitted to take the life of the unborn child. The second condition is that once the question has been weighed, the decision before God must be made courageously—conscientiously, but also with certainty. Third, the decision can be made only as a response to the command of God, and fourth, it must be made in the knowledge of and in faith in the forgiveness of God in Christ.[2]

The next question is euthanasia, and at this point Barth gives a definite "no." He sees no point at which it is possible to think that an exception could be made. Bearing with the weak is involved in the nature of human community. Life as a creature of God and as the vehicle for obedience can sometimes be unpleasant and can sometimes seem to us to be meaningless, but in the sight of God life is never unworthy of being lived. There is, however, what practically amounts to an exception even to this statement; it lies in the fact that modern medical science often has the means to prolong human lives artificially and uselessly. Here again, then, it might be possible to speak of an extreme case of "mercy killing" in the sense of a decision simply not to use to the utmost degree all the means which modern medical science makes available for the artificial prolongation of human life. This is notoriously a question which the

[2] We must note that of these four conditions, three have their locus not in the factual data underlying the ethical decision, but in the subjective attitude of the one deciding. They measure not the situation but how the person understands his decision. We shall have occasion to return to this slight "existentialistic" or "intentional" strand in Barth's thought.

progress of medical technology since 1950 has made all the more pressing.

A much more extensive section is the one which deals with human self-defense. Again Barth begins with a resounding insistence that there is no realm in which the Christian duty to return good for evil, to turn the other cheek, to go a second mile, does not apply. He puts himself in outright opposition to traditional Reformed and Lutheran theological ethics by clearly condemning those doctrines according to which there are certain areas in which a Christian would justifiably and normally defend himself even at the cost of the lives of others. It would have been one hundred times better if Christians in the past had erred in the direction of Tolstoy and Gandhi rather than in the direction of constructing apologies for the Christian use of violence in self-defense (*CD* 430). It is not true that every individual may properly ascribe to himself, whenever he needs it, the authority to carry out the police function of using violence for the preservation of order and, especially, for the preservation of his own skin. The life of the other person who threatens him is also in need of defense. It is no service to the cause of life to answer evil with evil. Both Jesus (Matt. 5:38-42) and Paul (I Cor. 6; Rom. 12) speak of the conscious and intentional abandon of one's legitimate rights and of self out of love. Barth says,

> These Gospel words belong to those of which it is said that they shall not pass away. They express precisely not just a well-intentioned exaggeration of some sort of humaneness or a special rule for good and especially good Christians. They express rather the command of God which is relevant and binding for all men, in the basic sense of that command and in the sense which *until further notice* must be taken to be final. (*KD* 491, italics mine; cf. *CD* 430.)

Yet we cannot make a law even of these words of the New Testament. "Further notice" is possible, though not in the sense that we can know ahead of time when we will be permitted to make exceptions. When it is not a matter of a conflict between two persons but rather of the salvation of order within human society in the interest of third parties, the use of force will possibly be necessary. This is the function of the state, of course. The fact that the state uses force in this way does not mean that the individual himself is generally, or automatically, authorized to use force in the name of the state to protect himself. Yet in the interest of that order of human togetherness which requires that the third parties be defended, the Christian could be called upon by the exceptional "further notice" of the command of God, in the extreme case, to take life.

Last in the series of questions preceding the problem of war, Barth discusses the death penalty. He refers to its origin in human history in traditions of tribal vengeance. He speaks, with evident regret and even shame, of the fact that the church in all its history never seemed to have any doubts about the necessity, the advisability, or even the goodness of the death penalty. It was left to the age of the Enlightenment to question fundamentally its justifiability.

There are logically three possible kinds of ground for judicial penalties. The first is the protection of society. But a protection which is so absolute as to require the absolute elimination of any menace is justifiable only if the state which is to be protected, or the nation which intends to protect itself, is also an absolute. The absolute value of the state or the human social order is, however, something which the Christian cannot affirm. The second general reason for penalties is the expiation of an offense against the moral order; yet the Christian knows that there can and need be no more expiation since the cross of Christ. The third general ground for judicial penalties is the argument that through punishment the criminal may be rendered a more useful citizen. In this case killing is conceivable only if we are sure ahead of time that no improvement is possible; this also is something which a Christian may not affirm. Thus Barth concludes that the death penalty normally is never acceptable; capital punishment may not legitimately be a state institution. However, in exceptional cases the death penalty might become a necessity. Such cases arise in wartime, e.g., as treason or perhaps as the necessity to assassinate a tyrant. Both these possibilities belong in the field of warfare rather than in the field of normal judicial procedure; we shall therefore defer their discussion.[3]

To almost every affirmation Barth offers an apparent exception. Before we follow Barth's dealing with the question of war, we must seek clearer understanding of the nature of the *concept* underlying the exceptions that may need to be made, or at least handled as open possibilities. Here

[3] Cf. below, pp. 37 ff. on war; p. 105, n. 3 on the death penalty.

Barth's own text may very well mislead unwary readers. Many a non-pacifist seeking to support his approval of war by appealing to Barth may, at this point, have burdened Barth's statements with a significance different from his intention.[4]

First of all, we face a linguistic problem. Barth's term for these exceptional cases is *Grenzfall,* literally translated, "borderline case," or "limiting case," or "extreme case." Yet the German term is not rendered precisely by any of these.

The *Grenzfall* does not mean that there must be an exception to every affirmation; nor does it mean to affirm in advance that, in a given case where certain conditions are met, the taking of life would be right. Such an interpretation would be a reversion to casuistry, which is precisely what Barth wants to avoid, though his disciples may go beyond his intent here. To understand the *Grenzfall* we must remember that bodily life, as one of the dimensions of human creatureliness, is good because it is the presupposition, the vehicle, so to speak, of obedience to God; but the "good" of life is for this reason not an absolute; it is not an autonomous value. "Not autonomous" means *limited* (*begrenzt*). The limit is God's purpose for life. The true measure of the goodness of life is obedience to the command of God. God is himself free to command as he wills; otherwise he would no longer be sovereign.

To be fully accurate, therefore, the *Grenzfall* is not a prediction that there can or will be an exception to the general rule in a specific case; it is rather a sort of double negative. It is not the statement that God will make exceptions, but the denial of man's right to refuse God the freedom to make exceptions if he so wills. The *Grenzfall* is thus not itself an exception but a form of faithfulness. It does not contradict what God originally said, but rather limits (again we come to the term "border") man's capacity and right to make affirmations about what God's Words mean.

How than can we understand the cases of which Barth has written where suicide or some other form of killing might be commanded? They are to be understood not as affirmations, although they are at times stated that way, but as illustrations answering the question which arises

[4] Here I am guided by *CD* II/2 and the fruit of personal conversation with Professor Barth—not only by the text of *KD* III/4 where the concept of the *Grenzfall* is used.

when Barth states that the duty to protect life is not an absolute principle. In the interest of clarity, Barth felt himself obliged to speak hypothetically of the conceivable places at which such an exception might be least unlikely. That God is sovereign, and remains sovereign over his command after he has spoken, is a statement which Barth makes on "systematic" grounds, i.e., because his general understanding of God and of the nature of revelation demands it. But then the reader asks, "What if God were to exercise this further freedom? What might he command?" It is to answer that implicit challenge, making the sovereignty of God concretely conceivable, that Barth seeks to project, on the far edge (*Grenze*) of the command's normal meaning, such a case.

In the second part of this book we shall ask whether this conception of the *Grenzfall* is stated with adequate clarity and especially whether, when properly understood, it is adequate for the use later made of it.

IV
Barth's Revision of the Traditional View of War

Barth now moves on to a merciless critique of the complacency and the good conscience with which traditional theology has always justified war. He is led to the vigor of this critique partly because it is no longer possible, as it once was, to be a spectator. It is no longer the state that wages war but the entire population and therefore every individual. All efforts to glorify war with some sort of mystical halo or flavor of chivalry must now be abandoned. We know that war is a matter of selfish interests; it is an economic matter. War is a symptom of the sickness of our "peacetime" life, a symptom of man's incapacity to master his situation and to organize a peace justly. War no longer means simply an attempt to neutralize the enemy, as may have been the case in some periods of human history. This is the point at which classic arguments justifying war are unrealistic. War's intention is not only to destroy the resistance of the enemy, but also to destroy the enemy himself. War destroys entire populations. War means "killing without glory, without dignity, without chivalry, without restraint, and without reserve" (*KD* 518; cf. *CD* 453).

It must therefore be absolutely clear that, if it may ever be necessary to speak of the *Grenzfall* of necessary participation in war, this can only be done "with even stricter reserve and caution" (*CD* 454) than has been observed in the consideration of other cases of killing. The fact that the soldier stands not merely side-by-side with the hangman or with the suicide but in fact even farther down the slope, cannot be hidden. The soldier is involved in an action which cannot be considered good, as commanded by God, except in that infinitely narrow border zone separated by a hair-thin line from murder.

War is more serious now than ever before, for three reasons. First, it involves everyone in the civil community. Not only is everyone the sufferer in war; everyone also inflicts suffering. Second, war is now more serious than ever before because the enemy, the man across the border, is guilty only for having the same loyalty to his cause, his nation, and his people that we have for ours. The man whom the soldier seeks to kill in warfare is not a guilty man in the sense that every soldier on the other side is a war criminal. He is simply a man who, like the soldier on the other side, has obeyed orders and accepted sacrifice and danger for the sake of his country. Third, war is more serious than any other kind of killing and is today more serious than it has ever been before because it involves all other sins. To wage war means not only to kill, but to kill without glory, without dignity, without chivalry, without limit, without reserve; it also means to steal, to ransack, to burn, to lie, to deceive, to dishonor, and to fornicate (*CD* 454). In spite of the heroism and discipline which wartime experience may mean for a few, war does not make men better. On the contrary, war for most men is unparalleled temptation.

Barth has here expressed a critique of war which is unique in the history of mainstream European Protestant theology. To say that war is worse than other kinds of killing already means a revolution in theological ethics. Protestants and Catholics alike have taught for centuries that abortion and suicide are far more serious kinds of killing than is warfare. In reversing the order of importance of these various kinds of disobedience to the order of God, Barth has already made a tremendous step toward a wholly new apprehension of the problem. He goes so far as to say that the rigorous refusal of war which one finds in pacifism, as he understands it (we shall need to ask later what his understanding is), "has almost infinite arguments in its favor and is almost overpoweringly strong" (*CD* 455). Pacifism thus is far nearer the truth than any other *general* ethical evaluation of war. The traditional acceptance of war as a normal instrument of national policy, going even so far as to make it part of the definition of the essence of the state, is for Barth an "increasingly unbearable perversion of Christian truth" (*CD* 455). It signifies a loss of Christian eschatology and an abdication before the state. True enough, the necessity of the state cannot be denied by Christian theology; yet the traditional Christian attitudes have gone far beyond the admission that the state is necessary. They have forgotten that even the state is necessary only provisionally, only in a subordinate way.

War is thus never normal. War is not essential to the state's function, but is rather foreign to what the state should be doing. Only as a last resort can one ever conceive of the possibility of war for the Christian. Never can the state be given *carte blanche*. The church's task is not to justify the use of force but to keep her distance from it. If the church as a matter of habit tolerates the use of force and planning for warfare on the part of the state, then she will not even know when the exceptional time has come when it would be justified for her to say a Christian "yes." Barth acidly exposes traditional theology's way of building into ethics the necessity of war. It was a type of theological thinking which intentionally made room for the historic vocation of the nation and thus provided the doctrinal scaffolding later used by the architects of World Wars I and II. It is one of the vestiges of the nineteenth-century conception of world history as a series of battles.

The normal function of the state is neither war nor readiness for war, but peace. First of all, the state's function is to maintain internal peace. War is a sign of the state's failure, because it means that peace has become injustice. Likewise the state's function is to maintain external peace. Neither pacifism nor militarism requires the exercise of much insight in weighing the cost and the prerequisites of external peace. What does require insight is to see that the main problem is what to *do* about keeping the peace. This is the message of the church to the state. What is needed is neither the pacifist insistence on disarmament nor the militarist insistence upon armament, but the elimination of occasions for war. The church cannot preach that war is always avoidable; still less can she be permitted to give the least expression to the satanic idea that war is unavoidable. She must and can proclaim at least that war is relatively avoidable, and that it is the responsibility of the state to carry that avoidance as far as humanly possible through the maintenance of justice. Only when this has been said and resaid, only when the great share of truth in the pacifist position has been admitted, can the church go on to affirm that Christian participation in war is not absolutely outside all possibility. At this point only will the church be justified in opposing the absolutism of the pacifist thesis. It is in the interest of the pacifist thesis, in fact, to see its limits. Consistency in the sense of absolute fidelity to a principle has not the same value in Christian ethics which it has in logic.

The question of warfare arises in the abnormal case when a people by the fault of another people, stands before a choice between disappearance and self-defense. Only in such a case is a decision in favor of war ever possible. Other reasons for war, including most of the reasons for which wars have been fought in the past—the idea of a nation's historic mission, the defense of international order against a menace implicit in the internal affairs of another state, or the defense of national honor—cannot be called upon to validate war with all that it costs (*CD* 461). Even the existence of a national state is not necessarily always worthy of military defense. One can imagine a case in which the church should advise a nation to submit to the enemy, as did Jeremiah. A legitimate war is conceivable only when it involves a nation's defense of its existence *within its own frontiers* and at a time when this nation has no right to run the risk of extinction.

But could such a reason be sufficient to permit calling a war, with all the horrors it must bring with it, a just war? It is, because the threat to a people's independence can involve that people's entire physical, moral, and spiritual existence, including its relationship to God. A people's responsibility for its existence may have been entrusted to it by God as a witness which it may not abandon. The existence of the state which binds together this particular people, with the justice of human community relations which is thereby assured, must in such a case be preferred even to the life of those who, unfortunately, menace it. It may be that God forbids the surrender of the independence of a state, without regard for the lives at stake. Christian ethics cannot deny that such a case may arise, for in a state of extremity it may be imposed by the commandment of God. As an example of this extremity, Barth notes that in his opinion the defense of the political independence or territorial integrity of the Swiss Republic would be such a case (*CD* 462).

The possibility of this case eliminates a consistent pacifism for Christian ethics. Not only does this case render possible the necessity of self-defense by one nation; it also makes it possible to justify the participation of other states in that war, if in doing so they come to the rescue of a state which is thus menaced and is thus legitimately defending itself. Finally, if war itself cannot be eliminated absolutely as a matter of principle from Christian ethics, neither can preparation for national defense be eliminated.

Barth adds what he calls a "distinctively Christian note" (*CD* 463). If a people is called by God to defend its national existence, then this defense must be carried on without regard for its effectiveness or success. The readiness of such a people to defend itself at all costs, even when there is no hope, will be the criterion of the state of necessity. As long as there can be calculation as to whether or not self-defense is likely to be successful, the people do not yet stand in the state of necessity.[1] Jeremiah's "defeatism" stood in the face of good chances for self-defense with the

[1] One of the strongest statements in this heroic tone is made in a wartime "Letter to an American": "The more calmly one sees and concedes that all of us in this war stand under God's judgment in the same way. . . , the more cold-bloodedly and energetically will the war be waged, because then one . . . will have a good conscience in this hard and terrible business." *Eine Schweizer Stimme, 1938-1945* (Zollikon-Zürich: Evangelischer Verlag, 1945), p. 279. This note of "good conscience" which links up with the readiness to die for a lost cause, is considered especially unevangelical by A. Th. van Leeuwen, "Oorlog als Ultima Ratio," in *Wending,* January 1953, pp. 619 ff.

The pacifist would have brought in the "distinctively Christian note" one step sooner and said that when there are only two apparent solutions, both evil, it might be "specifically Christian" to seek a third way, more costly but less evil. It is noteworthy that, for Barth, this "specifically Christian note" does not apply to the Christian's analysis of the situation or to his decision, but only to his courage and steadfastness in its execution. It is not a prerequisite for the decision's being right, but only a "note" concerning the Christian's state of mind. According to this thinking, a Christian does what any sane man would do in his place, but he does it with more courage and assurance.

help of Egypt. The church that has known how to direct the people to their internal and external duties in the defense of peace will also find in this state of extremity the message which will strengthen and guide a nation in the conduct of that rare war which, commanded by God, is not murder but a necessary killing.

V
Individual Responsibility and Military Service

Up to this point, Barth has been dealing with war as it concerns the state. But the state is made up of individuals, and every individual stands responsible before God. In war, too, therefore, responsibility cannot be avoided by the individual. Traditional theological ethics has unjustifiably personified and absolutized the state. This is bad not only for Christian ethics in general; it is especially bad for the state itself. The church must not only speak to the state, then, but she must ask every individual: Do you see the horror of war? Have you worked for peace?

Because this individual responsibility is unavoidable, compulsory military service is a good thing. It prevents anyone from thinking that he can avoid the problem of war—that is to say, the duty of peace—by leaving to others the unpleasant parts of that duty. To leave the defense of human order to others in such a way is not only pharisaism; it is a sure way to contribute to the prevalence of war. Yet this universal duty to serve is not a commandment of God but a commandment of the state, and therefore only a *question* which is posed to every individual. One cannot deny the exceptional possibility of a negative answer, i.e., of conscientious objection.

Conscientious objection to military service can be the right answer for an individual under two conditions: first, under the condition that the refusal of warfare be made and stated, not from the base of an anarchism which rejects the state as such, but in fidelity to the state's own highest purpose and calling. This will mean, naturally, that conscientious objection must be in every case a decision of the moment, based on evaluation of the particular war in question and not a refusal of all wars. The conscientious objector is therefore in error if his rejection covers all war in principle. Absolutism in any field of ethics is revolt against the divine order. It is shutting oneself off from the command of the living God. The refusal of military service is possible, then, only if one does not deny that the state may in some circumstances make and prepare war. Valid conscientious objection must include the readiness to decide otherwise at another time. Only thus does one respect God's freedom to speak ever anew to man; only thus does one retain one's own freedom to hear him. Second, conscientious objection is conceivably justified only if the conscientious objector is himself ready to accept the suffering which his deviance will bring upon him. He has no right to request exceptional treatment because of the fact that he is driven by conscience.

The refusal of military service, though it cannot be made an absolute, has thus become a real possibility—one which is increasingly likely in our time. The state cannot provide a law for the general recognition of all conscientious objection (especially, we may add, if such objection must be based upon a differing way of weighing the political aspects of a given war, rather than on absolute principle)[1] but the government should nevertheless learn to reckon with the eventuality of a point where perhaps not only individual exceptional Christians but even Christians as a

[1] Switzerland has been among the slowest of the Western democracies to provide any legal recognition even for the kind of conscientious objector who rejects all wars. Barth does not speak here to this question. He rejects such "absolutist" objection as theologically wrong and gives no attention to how a government should treat the holders of such erroneous views. He does not admit the validity of absolutist objection even as a special vocation or a prophetic sign. His denial of the feasibility of governmental provision for objectors here refers to what has since come to be called the "selective objector," a category which American draft legislation has always rejected.

body could be led by the call of God to refuse to participate in war. Not only should the state be ready to face such a possibility; much more should the church in her pastoral work consider it as something which might, even should, sometime happen. The church should stop teaching the absolute duty of military service and should teach the duty of individual, conscientious decision. Further, since the necessary war is very rare and cannot in fact be seen and decided upon in advance, the church should always be ready to enter corporately the ranks of the opposition, expressing her faithfulness to what the state *should be* through her insubordination to what the state *is*. The church must be ready to suffer and to take upon herself all that would be involved in a collective act of conscientious objection. If the state knew that the church is really reserving for herself the freedom to refuse to participate, the state would thereby be made aware of the danger of injustice which is at the same time the state's *raison d'être* and the state's own particular temptation.

In speaking of the church's political responsibility, we have already mentioned the universality of human responsibility for the state. "The infamous statement attributed to Louis XIV can and should be corrected. Every individual in his own place and function is the state" (*CD* 464). We noted before that Barth considers universal military service as a healthy thing because it extends to everyone the necessity of deciding what he shall do about the question posed by war. For Barth, this political responsibility of the church and of the Christian is not a matter of debate; it is not up to us to ask whether it is good or bad that the Christian, or that every man, is responsible for the state. It is a simple fact that there is no possibility of avoiding responsibility. He who seeks to avoid responsibility by expressing no opinion, whether he does so in the form of refusing to vote or by separating himself from the political arena in some broader sense, simply supports the stronger party. In case of war, which is the critical case, anyone who would attempt to avoid his political responsibility by saying "no" to Swiss self-defense or who would attempt simply to take no position, would really be taking sides for the aggressor. There is no way to be neutral, for war is total, nor is there any other way to resist, once things have gone that far, than to oppose violence with violence. The civilian *is* the soldier; the voter *is* the government executive. There is a division of functions but not of responsibility.

For Barth, then, the Christian's responsibility for political order involves basically the duty to defend the brute existence of the state. That the state exists belongs to the order of God (cf. Rom. 13). Even though its mission is only secondary, subordinate in value to that of the church, as Barth says very clearly, it is nevertheless necessary. Its necessity includes that of violence and, in the extreme case, of military violence. To reject all violence would be to deny the legitimacy of the state. Especially for the Western democracies—e.g., Switzerland, the Netherlands, the Scandinavian countries, France, England—this responsibility for the legitimacy of the state takes on the form of defense of democracy. The existence of democracy, which itself is a product of the gospel and which must be evaluated as a good thing, means that the Christian's duty is not only passive submission to the state—which is all that Romans 13 requires expressly—but also a share of positive responsibility for the existence of the state and for the active fulfillment of the state's own responsibility, including its duty to protect its own existence. This does not mean that there is an end to the "stranger and pilgrim" status of the Christian in the world. Nor does it mean that there will be an end to the Christian's freedom to criticize the state and its decisions. It means simply that the only way of making meaningful a critique of the state in the modern world is to express that critique through the acceptance, the preservation, and the utilization of democratic instruments of government.

VI
The Structure of Decision

The specific issue which Barth raises in connection with his definition of God's freedom and the statement that killing is permissible, not when or because certain conditions are met, but when and because God commands it, emerges in the question: Whence and how does this commandment come? At every point in his exposition with relation to suicide, to abortion, and still more clearly with relation to the question of war, Barth affirms that only the command of God can tell us when we stand before the *Grenzfall.* There is only one command of God, and that command is spoken to man in Jesus Christ. Because there is only one command, there can be no casuistry, no encyclopedia of all possible Christian decisions prepared in advance. Because there can be no casuistry, man stands in every decision before God and is called to hear God's Word and to obey. Here and now God speaks to man in judgment and in grace and thereby also in command. In God's sovereign freedom, which is his grace, God speaks to man where he is and gives him for his time and place a commandment which he is to hear and to carry out without further question.

This could be said by someone whose ethic is based upon mysticism or upon intuition. It could be said by someone incapable of distinguishing between his own momentary feelings and the command of God. We may be tempted to ask whether Barth himself has an "intuitionist" conception of the command of God—and it is surprising that he has gone to so little trouble to ward off such a misunderstanding. For Christian ethics to be a "science," as Barth considers it, there must be some way of "testing the spirits," some way of knowing whether and when that which an individual thinks God told him is really the Word of God. What is the test which protects us against arbitrary subjectivism?

Our hearing God's Word is not a private matter. To hear God's Word the Christian will listen to the apostles and prophets. He will listen to Jesus Christ, as the apostles and prophets testify to him. He will listen to the Christian church as it testifies to Jesus Christ. He will give account to his contemporaries and to his posterity. He will be ready before and after his decision to examine the reasons for his choice. This conversation which he carries on with the Christian past and with his contemporaries cannot be codified, and yet, since there is one God and one Word, it will be possible to find the main lines of Christian thinking about decision. This is the science of ethics. Ethics is not the process of Christian decision, but the evaluation of the reasons presented for decision, as the Christian converses, before and after his decision, with the Christian past and with the Christian brotherhood. We cannot judge whether a Christian's act is right or wrong, but we can call upon him to account for the decision he has made by presenting for examination, and for testing by the criterion of the Word of God, his reasons for deciding as he did.

But how, then, is his decision made? The Word of God in the situation, in this conversation with the Christian past and the Christian present, comes neither by intuition nor through a pietistic or pentecostal experience of "revelation." It is not to be equated with the "guidance" which the enthusiasts of Moral Re-Armament receive "from the blue." It comes in man's standing before his problem, in his seeking a full and accurate understanding of the situation in which his choice must be made, in the evaluation of all the available alternative ways of acting, and in the choice which he then makes in prayer, in conversation, in faith, but also in the full use of his intelligence. The choice is made between the available alternatives, and the Christian chooses simply what appears to be best, or the least evil. When Barth speaks thus of the Word which God addresses to a specific situation, he in no way means some kind of new superhuman channel of inside information whereby the Christian would receive a new truth specifically for his time and place. Barth means rather that the human search for the good or the best possibility,[1] carried on within man's limitations and with the use of man's faculties, is the context in which man is called upon to hear God and to obey. The best possible choice will be the result of—or rather will be the same as—hearing God's specific Word to a specific time and place. As in any other area of Christian faith, we stand here before a leap to be taken in the midst of ambiguities. The Christian must make his own decision in prayer and in faith and then go on in the confidence that that decision was brought about by God himself, just as in belief itself the Christian comes to confess his faith humanly and consciously but does not ascribe that faith to his own choice but to God working in him. The language which portrays God as speaking in the situation must not be understood as in disjunction from sober pragmatic calculation.

Therefore the political situation, an exact knowledge of what was going on and what were the possible and available ways of acting, preoccupied Karl Barth not only in fact—we know the history of his own interest in politics—but also in theory. Here again we can best illustrate by example.[2]

[1] "We must choose the best possibility and not hesitate, but act with good conscience" (John Godsey, ed., *Karl Barth's Table Talk* [Richmond, Va.: John Knox Press, 1963], p. 80). Against a certain Lutheran or Niebuhrian tendency to think of a given deed (e.g. killing or lying) as a "necessary evil" to be committed repentantly, Barth insists that such a deed (the same deed, even though it be hurtful to someone) is not evil but good. Thus he does not favor the *label* "lesser evil" with which such a weighing of "the best possibility" is usually designated. But his reason for not using the term relates to his conviction that the "less evil" action as "the best possibility" in the given situation, is not sinful. Barth does not thereby place ethics in another ultimate context than that of the calculation of the less harmful results. Cf. below, pp. 83 ff., on the "lesser evil" logic.

[2] The first certain trumpet blast against Hitler was Barth's letter addressed to Joseph Hromádka upon the invasion of Czechoslovakia, saying that Czechoslovakian soldiers resisting Hitler's invasion would be fighting for Christ and his church. (Letter of Sept. 19, 1938, in K. Barth, *Eine Schweizer Stimme, 1938-1945,* pp. 58-59).

Cf. also, K. Barth, *This Christian Cause* (New York: The Macmillan Co., 1941). However, the Hromádka letter should not be taken as the prime specimen of Barth's pro-war thought because (a) the call to Czechoslovak resistance was linked in an unclear way to

Switzerland is threatened by Hitler, and a knowledge of the situation tells us that the Third Reich is a demonic state in which injustice is not simply an accident but a principle. No such state has the right to exist. Switzerland, on the other hand, is a state based upon justice, which in spite of all its imperfections and all its disobedience to God's commands still admits in its constitution and in its daily administration that justice must be served.

Barth distinguishes between the "just state" (*gerechter Staat*) and the "justice-state" (*Rechtsstaat*). Whether a state is just in its constitution and administration is a relative matter. Injustice may and does occur in Switzerland. But whether or not a state is committed to executing justice, i.e., whether or not it recognizes an obligation to norms above itself, is not a relative matter. It can be measured in the formal commitments of both persons and structures. On this level there is no questioning the qualitative difference between Switzerland and Hitler's Germany.

Thus, in case of attack, the choice is to defend Switzerland at the cost of German and Swiss lives or to abandon the existence of a justice-state (*Rechtsstaat*) before the invasion of an unjust state or anti-state. The best choice available is to defend by war, and therefore to be prepared before the attack to defend by war, the existence of the Swiss state which guarantees to the Swiss people this relatively great degree of justice, rather than to surrender the order of that state before the menace of another order which in its very foundation is nothing but disorder.

There is, therefore, something worse than war, and that is the full abandon of the state itself. Forced to decide in 1938, in 1940, or in 1943 whether Switzerland should be ready to defend itself or be ready to abandon its existence, the Swiss Christian had to choose, and Karl Barth did choose, the lesser evil. It is the only path available, and therefore in faith he must have the courage to believe simply, sincerely, and totally that this is the Word of God to his time. His decision is made in the knowledge that all human decisions are imperfect, that all human existence is involved in sinfulness, and that if God accepts this decision or any decision as having been right, it is only in his grace.

---

unrealistic political prognostications about the hope that, if Prague's troops could hold the line, London and Paris might also resist; (b) although he defended that utterance in the wartime period, Barth in his later systematic writing did not choose to use it as a specimen. The Swiss case is the only specimen provided in *CD* III/4.

VII
Pacifisms Old and New

In an account of the encounter between Karl Barth's position and that of Christian pacifism in general, we must first of all weigh the full significance of the fact that Karl Barth is the only European theologian of his stature in modern times to have gone as far as he did toward the position he criticizes. He declares the pacifist case to be "almost overpowering," even though he cannot accept it fully. Barth's rejection of pacifism is a rejection which has listened attentively to much of what Christian pacifism is trying to say. This degree of understanding is all the more striking when one considers that Barth's acquaintance with the theological basis of Christian pacifism seems to have been limited, at the time he wrote Volume III/4, to three sources: the heritage of Leo Tolstoy, an early acquaintance with Swiss pacifists of the school of Leonhard Ragaz, and one book by G. J. Heering.[1] Both the Heering book and the Ragaz contacts dated from the nineteen-twenties.

[1] G. J. Heering, *De Zondeval van het Christendom,* 1928, trans. by J. W. Thompson as *The Fall of Christianity* (London: G. Allen & Unwin, 1930; American reprint by Fellowship Publications, New York, 1943).

The degree to which Barth has understood and in fact agreed with pacifism demonstrates that he is misunderstood when he is interpreted to confirm the traditional rejection of pacifism by Christian theologians. Karl Barth is far nearer to Christian pacifism than he is to any kind of systematic apology for Christian participation in war. For him it is theologically not possible to construct a justification of war. There is no Christian argument for participating in war. There is only the possibility of "limiting cases," whose sole ground is God's sovereign (and exceptional) command to man.

The discussion with Barth is therefore not a debate between pacifism and militarism, nor even between pacifism and non-pacifism. It is rather a debate to be carried on within the pacifist camp, between one position which is pacifist in all the general statements it can make but announces in advance that it is willing to make major exceptions, and another position, nearly the same in theory, which is not able to affirm in advance the possibility of the exceptional case.

Our first problem as we proceed from description to critique is to define what that "pacifism" is which we contrast with Barth's "relative pacifism." Barth's position we know, even if one may argue that it has changed slightly with time and leaves some issues open; but what is the other position with which it is to be contrasted?

Barth himself never describes clearly the "pacifism" which he rejects; what he understands it to be is inferred in his negative arguments. He seems to assume that both he and his readers understand exactly what he means by the term.[2] At only one point, namely, in his rejection of

[2] Most of Barth's allusions to "pacifism" presuppose that he and his readers have already rejected it, and then ask that those who reject it do so not hastily, without hearing the "almost infinite argument in its favor." Yet those arguments in its favor are never exposited from the history of Christian pacifism. Many of Barth's students have learned from him how to read appreciatively Luther or Calvin, Schleiermacher or Sartre, Augustine or Anselm. Yet there is no effort here to hear the witness of Tertullian or Peter of Cheltchitz, of Fox or Tolstoy. This is all the more striking in view of the way pacifism is taken as a paradigm of the whole ethical problem. Killing, and not adultery or lying, is the obvious example appealed to in the statement of the paradoxical goodness of the divine command (*CD* II/2, 712). Killing, not marriage or work or truth-telling, is the issue around which the *Grenzfall* concept must be developed. The problem of tyranny and war, not contraception or education or economics, was the theme of Barth's major involvement in politics. Yet nowhere does he develop inductively for his reader a sense of what the Christian pacifist tradition has been about over the centuries. He grants "almost infinite weight" to a position which he has not (as far as the record shows) studied at any depth.

consistent "principles," does he speak directly of "pacifism" as he conceives it; even there his rejection of "pacifism" is a decision with which he begins rather than a conclusion growing out of the exposition.[3] The following traits seem to be characteristic of the "pacifists" whose position he opposes:

1. The "pacifist" is a legalist. He has answered all questions before they are asked, by virtue of an inflexible and impersonal formal principle which he is incapable of examining further and which dispenses him from any further need to listen to God.
2. The "pacifist" believes that the state easily can and immediately should abandon violence.
3. The "pacifist's position is not specifically Christian; his models are Tolstoy and Gandhi, and he proposes his "ism" as a secular humanist ethical guide for non-Christian societies.
4. If the "pacifist" makes any claim to hold a distinctively Christian position, he bases that claim on ethical "principles" drawn from the Decalogue or the Sermon on the Mount, such as the commandment according to which killing is forbidden. These principles, though enunciated by Jesus, would in the mind of the "pacifist" also be valid without him. They can and should be applied absolutely without exception.

Our present purpose is not to provide a survey of modern pacifist movements or literature. It need only be said that the above description is in no way typical of the kind of theologically defended Christian pacifism which today asks a hearing.

Any serious analysis of the varieties of theological pacifisms would need to distinguish clearly among at least the following types[4]:

[3] *CD* III/4, 468; the parallel with an "absolutist militarism" is formal. What Barth here condemns is a particular style in ethics, which he calls "absolutist," and not the substance of a particular pacifist stance. Only by some semantic quirk would it be possible to argue (as Barth does not, but some "situationist" anti-pacifists do) that the rejection of war is more rigid or more legalist than the other alternatives; war demands by definition a powerful legal, institutional, budgetary base, as rigid as one can imagine.

[4] In a later study I hope to be able to disentangle and interpret a score of "Varieties of Pacifism." It is just as questionable to lump all rejectors of war under one heading as it is confusing to group Barth, Brunner, Bonhoeffer, and the Niebuhr brothers as "neo-orthodox." It is as illogical to assume all pacifists are legalist, or naïve, or socially irresponsible, as it is to assume that all Swiss yodel, just because some of them do.

ecclesiologically oriented rejection of war, as part of a "radical reformation" vision of the relation of church and society, as represented by the historic peace churches;

ethically oriented pacifism, i.e., discussion and rejection of participation of war as a moral issue which can be discussed in its own right within the framework of a given theological tradition. Within Barth's own Reformed tradition the most competent expressions are:

in exegetical terms, G. H. C. MacGregor's *The New Testament Basis of Pacifism;* Fellowship Publications, New York, numerous editions since 1936;

in doctrinal terms, Jean Lasserre's *War and the Gospel,* 1953 (English ed., Scottdale, Pa.: Herald Press, 1962).

humanistically oriented pacifism, proceeding from a stance not limited to Christian language and loyalty, yet often deeply integrated into biblical faith: characteristic of some modern Quakers and of many individuals within the nonpacifist denominations, as well as of numerous Jews;

"just war pacifism," driven by careful respect for the moral tradition which once permitted war only under very carefully controlled cases, to a total a priori rejection of any war that is conceivable in our time, since by the nature of modern military reality it could not possibly meet the requirements;

anarchist pacifism, which in the "Christian" form represented by Jehovah's Witnesses has been the position of most of the conscientious objectors in French, Swiss, and German jails.

With none of these does Barth deal directly. Heering's *Fall of Christianity* may be considered as representing a fusion of the "ethical" and the "humanistic." Heering is cited but not dealt with directly.

In discussing "pacifism" in this context, then, we do not need to defend all the positions which Barth attacks but merely define the kind of "pacifism" with which we intend to confront Barth's "non-pacifism." The rejection of war is not limited to any particular theology, nor to the major types listed above; it is found among Waldensians, Franciscans, the "left wing" of the Reformation, Quakers, Methodists, Tolstoians, and modern liberals. Contemporary individual Anglicans, Calvinists, and Lutherans, Pentecostals, and Kimbanguists have stood for "pacifism," each within the framework of their own doctrinal orientations. To advocate, in this critique of Barth, any particular one of these positions would only confuse matters, since then we would be dealing not primarily with the question of war, but with the conflicting underlying theological systems.

The only feasible approach is then to speak in terms of what might be called a "Barthian pacifism," seeking to meet Barth's arguments within the framework of his own system, accepting the norms and the understanding of the task of Christian ethics which he prescribes, and then asking whether his view of war as eventually possible is consistent with his own standards. This does not mean acceptance of Barth's theology, but rather limiting our arguments to those which he himself would logically have had to consider valid, even if certain basic criticism must be omitted by this limitation. As a result of this limitation our arguments will have to be less positive, longer, and polemically less impressive than if we were to construct a counterposition which would have to be Anabaptist, or humanist, or Catholic, or some other, and would only confuse this study.

Rather than attempting to make an extensive case for pacifism, we shall only ask whether Barth's own case has been made. "Pacifism" shall henceforth be used to signify nothing more precise than the inability of certain Christians to see how their participation in war could be a Christian imperative; we shall ask Barth only whether he has demonstrated that such an imperative can exist.

To speak in Barth's own terms will mean three things for our study:

1. The norm of theology is the revelation of God in Jesus Christ. Other considerations such as arguments from Christian tradition, from "nature" or "self-evidence," or from philosophical ethics, have no place as ultimate standards; a large part of the task of theology is to counteract the autonomy of such extraneous elements of thought.

2. Ethics is part of dogmatics. It has sometimes been suggested by commentators that in making this claim about ethics as a discipline, Barth has assigned to ethics an unusually modest place; in reality the opposite is the case. Instead of being a branch of empirical anthropology, describing how men *do* behave, or of philosophy, describing how they *think* they *should* behave, ethics becomes a part of the science which interprets the Word of God as to how man *must* or *shall* or *may* behave in free response to God's sovereign grace. Ethics participates fully in the

bindingness and the objectivity of the "queen of the sciences," for it deals not simply with man as he is, but with Jesus Christ, perfect Man, God's first and last Word to man.[5]

3. Christian ethics must respect fully the concrete situation in which man hears the call to obedience; valid ethical discourse is inseparable from accurate knowledge of historical realities and of the available alternatives.

Rather than challenging these axioms, or testing their limits, we shall posit them, agree with Barth that they point in the general direction of the rejection of all war, and then ask whether Barth is consistent with them when he does not follow them that far.

[5] See below, pp. 79 ff., 111 ff.

VIII
The Case Against Casuistry

The difference between Barth and Christian pacifism as he sees it lies not in the general conviction that war is wrong, but in Barth's readiness to foresee exceptions to the generally admitted wrongness of war. (We use the term "exception" here in its formal sense, not losing from sight, however, Barth's claim that what is apparently formally an exception is actually a deeper faithfulness to the law, the most concrete form of obedience.)

It would be pointless to argue further about the intrinsic wrongness of war, as one would have to do against a proponent of a traditional Catholic, Lutheran, or Calvinist position, for on this level Barth agrees with the pacifist. The remaining object of investigation, which must be approached with considerable care, is thus the methodology with which Barth's ethics permits that exception. The question falls normally into two parts: (1) What is the nature and validity of ethical generalizations, such as the statement that war is wrong? (2) What is the nature and validity of an exception which may be envisaged as commanded by God? If the exception can be affirmed, it must be either because the generalization is by nature not universally valid, or because there exist special grounds for nullifying its application in the extreme case. We turn first to the question: Are there general ethical commands that are universally valid?

Barth argues against the general formal validity of moral commands, even such commands as those of the Decalogue or the Sermon on the Mount. He does not deny that such commands express the will of God, but they do so as "samples" or "indications" of what obedience will mean when God speaks, and not as formal imperatives to be applied mechanically. This distinction is one of the major arguments brought forth in Barth's prolegomena to ethics (*CD* II/2), and we cannot deny its significance as a safeguard against the ossification of ethics into a rigid legalism. We must, however, ask to what extent and in what ways this distinction in terms is a real distinction in fact: Is it primarily a matter of terminology, or does it lead clearly to a difference in method which may be expected to have real significance for application in Christian ethics?

If we ask this question, we can see that the distinction which Barth makes between "indications" and "laws" is useful (1) when we are discussing the degree of literalism with which these directives are to be translated into action. The distinction is very relevant (2) when we are discussing the amount of liberty we have in adapting the directives to the realities of a new situation. In this sense the distinction which Barth makes is justified and useful. But if we agree with this and then move on to ask the next question, the one which preoccupies us at the present moment, the lay of the land is no longer so clear. When we ask, (3) "Do we have definite grounds for knowing that there will be exceptions to the general directive?" we are forced to conclude that Barth's distinction is not helpful.

Nowhere in the discussions of "the definiteness of the Word of God" does Barth spell out by what procedures he intends to "test the spirits." Analysis of the *implicit* procedures in concrete usage shows us three possibilities, each logically quite understandable:

a. There is the option of strict and logical casuistry, such as he applies most thoroughly in the case of abortion.

b. There is the option of reasonable projection; one chooses the "best possibility" among those which the amateur political scientist any modern man is expected to be, can see would come to pass if . . . . These are the options we have to deal with, most carefully. Yet there is a third possibility:

c. There is the test of the courage to go through with the action commanded in the *Grenzfall.* (Barth concludes that the attempted assassination of Hitler on July 20, 1944, was probably not commanded by God because the conspirators lacked the courage to carry it out as planned.[1]) Knowing the will of God is a matter of feeling one's emotional pulse.

By whichever of these means we may hold that the precise meaning of the will of God becomes clear to us, the distinction between "law" and "direction" is not determinative in the decision. Whether "thou shalt not kill" or "thou shalt not hate" is a "law" in some strict formal sense or simply an "indication" makes no difference. Neither the "law" nor the "indication" gives us any grounds for making a bridge to the opposite statement, "thou shalt kill for the sake of life." The statement that the "directive" in the Sermon on the Mount, for one example, is not legalistically binding still gives no grounds for saying that the Christian should in the extreme case do just the contrary of what is there "directed." This is, however, precisely what Barth claims we must affirm. What we must hold the door open for is not a loophole or a soft edge on the imperative, but a firm counterimperative.

If Barth is to come to the firm directive, "thou shalt take life," he must ground it by saying something like, "Take life for the sake of life," or, "Take life for the sake of the survival of the state," thus bringing back into the argument something suspiciously like another generally valid "principle," namely the value attributed to that for whose sake one must when necessary kill. In fact this argument involves two value judgments; first the desirability of "life," and then the claim, which is both theologi-

[1] "The plan miscarried simply because no one was prepared to go through with it in absolute disregard of his own life" *CD* III/4, 449). Barth goes on to argue that the case for justifiable tyrannicide was amply made according to the classical casuistic criteria. "In such a situation it might well have been the command of God." In other words, the command is more likely to come when the casuistic conditions are met, but the command is not the same as the conditions. "The only lesson to be learned is that they had no clear and categorical command from God to do it." Or perhaps they did, "but they failed to hear it." At this point a new variable enters in: the Command of God, coinciding with the casuistic conditions for killing, may have been there, but if it was, it was not heard.

cally and historically open to question, that the taking of one life can really be "for the sake of life." It is not within our immediate concern to go further and ask whether, as Barth takes for granted, remaining uncommitted by refusing to accept "principles" is actually in itself a sign of greater "responsibility." Here we only ascertain that to change our understanding of the Sermon on the Mount, in order to say that it is not a direct legal prescription, still gives no justification for the affirmation that it will not be binding in every case or that there will be cases in which we can say God commands us to do otherwise. The proof for that still needs to be brought. Barth's attack upon pharisaical conceptions of consistency or upon the general formal validity of ethical statements, within or without the Bible, justified as it may be in its place, is in itself not the needed proof.

The question may also be stated in another way, as it is in Barth's attack (in *CD* II/2, esp. section 38/2) against casuistry: Is it possible or desirable for Christian ethics to be consistent? Is it possible or desirable to apply general value judgments in such a way as to know, for a specific ethical choice, what is the intention of God?

Barth's critique of casuistry, which goes very far, still does not face this problem in the pure form. He does not clearly ask whether it is possible to make general statements about good behavior which could have the same validity in ethics as a statement about the divinity of Christ can have in theology. He faces only wrong kinds of casuistry and is able to reject them on grounds which, though valid, are not directly relevant to our question. He asks, "Can we say that a given act is always forbidden?" That is the question which is asked by that particular type of casuistry which we generally call "pharisaic." The "Pharisee," to use that term as Christians have defined it by caricature, has built a series of rules as to what is forbidden, and seeks to justify himself by abstaining from it. There is a second kind of casuistry which is generally identified, also through caricature, with the Jesuit. The "Jesuit," too, asks, "Is this act forbidden?" Then he finds ways for saying that, although it is forbidden, he may commit the act and still be justified.

Both these kinds of casuistry deal with how one may be justified by one's acts, by one's commission or omission of certain defined deeds. Both deal with the question of how to have a good conscience. The Protestant counterthesis is clear: to have a good conscience, casuistry is of no help.

But this is an entirely different matter from the kind of casuistry which deals seriously with conceivable cases in which the person who rejects all war, or, equally if not more so, the person who rejects some wars, is engaged. With this Barth does not deal; he is not concerned with the casuistry which does not seek justification but obedience, which does not seek to know what is forbidden but which asks what is commanded. This is a question with which Barth simply does not grapple. He attacks the casuistic argument of the good conscience with considerable vigor in a way with which we at present have no reason to disagree. But his attack on the casuistic argument of the good conscience fails precisely to answer the question that concerns us: Why should it not be possible for a general statement in Christian ethics to have the same validity as a general statement within some other realm of Christian dogmatics?[2]

This incompleteness on the part of Barth's critique of casuistry makes it easier for us to understand the basis on which he rejects pacifism. He rejects pacifism as if it were based upon a casuistry of conscience, in which the pacifist is expected to say, "Thou shalt not participate in war," and to promise that he who does not participate in war will thereby be justified before God. If this were the true Christian pacifist position (and Barth really seems to think it is), it would be demolished by Barth's argument. But that is not what Christian pacifism in any relevant form today is saying. Nor is accepting war a sure defense against such a view of ethics; the soldier's willingness to serve can also be considered a virtue before God.

The pacifist argues rather that, since Christian ethics is a matter of command and not prohibition, he is concerned in his ethics not with having a good conscience, but with being obedient. Therefore, the question is really: On what grounds does anyone advocate, as being positive

[2] In discussing the "definiteness of the divine decision" (*CD* II/2, 661 ff.), Barth favorably refers to the work of Eduard Thurneysen on *The Sermon on the Mount* (original 1936; trans. by W. C. Robinson and James M. Robinson [Richmond, Va.: John Knox Press, 1964]), but Thurneysen does not elaborate on the issue. In the early pages of III/4 Barth renews the encounter with casuistics and makes a greater effort to recognize the element of validity in the casuistic tradition. But it is progressively less clear just how the rejected "casuistics" differs from what Barth himself will be doing later with the *Grenzfall.*

Christian obedience, any other action than that which is consistent with the general line of Christian revelation? The grounds have yet to be brought forward; the pacifist who in his ethics claims to be bound to the general line of God's revelation without being able or authorized to predict exceptions is no less free *for obedience* than the theologian who in dogmatics is also bound to the general line of God's revelation in an affirmation about the nature of Christ or about the essence of the church. Only if the pacifist were dealing with an ethic of prohibition and of justification would Barth's claim that the pacifist is not a free Christian man be fitting.

We must in fact go one step further and realize that Barth himself resorts to casuistry when he introduces the concept of the "extreme case" and where he treats the problem of war. The extreme *case* is a concept of cas-uistry. When Barth explains what he means by the "extreme case" and gives examples, when he tells us that the place at which abortion is permitted is the point at which one life would have to be weighed against another, or when he says that the point at which war might be commanded by God is where the lives of enemy soldiers have to be weighed against the existence of a just state—those are casuistic arguments. If casuistry, in the sense of deduction from valid general value judgments including concern for their overlapping or conflict with other values, were to be completely eliminated, then there would be no reason why the extreme case (*Grenzfall*) should be at the border (*Grenze*). There would be no reason why abortion should not at some time be commanded by God when *no* mother's welfare is at stake, no reason why war on the death penalty should not be commanded by God when the state is *not* at stake. If God's sovereignty rejects all our calculations, there is no reason why I should not kill my nation's enemy when my people's freedom to worship God is *not* at stake. The fact that the only examples Barth can find of conceivable extreme cases are precisely *extreme cases,* where in the nature of the situation one value seems to be competing with another, is a demonstration that he cannot escape casuistry.[3]

The real concern of the casuistry of obedience is Barth's own concern,

[3] Not only does Barth not avoid casuistic reasoning; he in fact uses it in its least fruitful, negative-permissive form. He does not finally ask, "How can one in every situation testify in action to the relevance of God's having reconciled the world to himself in Christ?" but rather, "Is killing always forbidden?"

namely, fully to respect the situation. The *case* to which casuistry applies its general criteria is precisely the situation. Casuistry in the history of ethical thought is "situation ethics" par excellence. It differs from what is today popularly called "situation ethics" in that it comes to the situation prepared with certain criteria derived from the Christian community's past experience with God's revelation, instead of coming empty-handed and deciding extemporaneously on the basis of the possibilities and interests which seem in the moment to be at stake.

The question therefore is not whether or not to use casuistry, but whether or not the casuistic process with which one attempts to evaluate a decision is being manipulated fairly, in honest realization of its limitations, in clarity as to its norms, with flexibility to meet new situations, and with a constant readiness to submit every value judgment to the examination of one's brothers. Barth's critique of casuistry has not contributed to the demonstration that there can a priori be exceptions to the general rule concerning which he and pacifists agree. Barth's condemnation of the pacifist as one who is not a free human person led us to expect such an a priori case for exceptions, but that expectation was wrong. Any exception must be proven *in situ.*

IX
The *Grenzfall* as a Tool of Ethical Thought

While Barth gives us no *general* reasons for expecting a *Grenzfall,* he affirms exceptions on *specific* grounds which now need to be examined. So far we were asking whether the general argument against casuistry pulled the door open for authorized killing, on the grounds of generally correct ways of thinking; now we ask whether the *Grenzfall* pushes it open on the grounds of a concrete imperative. We must first ask whether the concept of the *Grenzfall* with which Barth here works is a concept whose utility in ethics has been made clear. Is it a workable, usable, and meaningful instrument in ethical thinking? Is it clear, is it unequivocal, and can it be guided by Christian revelation? In Barth's own arguments there are several different ways of using this concept. These several ways are not necessarily consistent with one another. We must therefore identify each of these different meanings and proceed to evaluate each of them before coming to a conclusion as to whether any of them, all of them, or a mixture of them may be legitimately used in carrying on the argument.

First of all, we encounter the phenomenon which Barth calls the *Grenzfall* in the form of what almost seems to be a solid principle: namely in the form of the rejection of all principles, a rejection stated so clearly that it takes the form of the general rule that there must be an exception to every rule. In this sense one of Barth's sympathetic interpreters has spoken of the *Grenzfall* as a "theological necessity," i.e., as a formal safeguard against taking any human utterance with too much total seriousness. In the unfolding of Barth's argument concerning the various kinds of killing, he considers first the general rule: "Thou shalt not kill." He argues strongly that the command of God is relevant in this field. Then he asks whether there can be an exception and, if so, where we should go to find it. This is done with the obvious expectation—seemingly almost for posited systematic reasons—that rules have exceptions. The exception (or at least its possibility) is in advance affirmed, or at least expected, for reasons drawn not so much from the nature of the case or from the content of Christian revelation or from an unequivocal Word of God here and now, as simply from Barth's presupposition that there can be no valid generalization. He expects in advance an exception as a theological possibility, which the structure of his argument forces him to weigh at every step. This expectation emerges repeatedly in the argument on abortion, self-defense, etc. The *Grenzfall* does not emerge unpredicted at a point where concrete problems turn out on inspection to be otherwise insoluble; the concrete cases are, rather, found to fit the place prepared for them by the systematic exposition.

Barth recognizes this when he is challenged about the critical fine-print passage where he says he would consider a war for the defense of the territorial integrity and political freedom of the Swiss Confederation to be commanded by God. He agrees that it is not theologically possible to make such an affirmation ahead of time.[1] The prediction is proffered only as a sample, as a hypothesis, to answer the challenge of people who

[1] This denial of the possibility of prediction contradicts the apparent clear sense of the text: "I may remark in passing that I myself should see it as such a case if there were any attack on the independence, neutrality and territorial integrity of the Swiss Confederation. . . (*CD* III/4, 462)." This corrective is brought with Prof. Barth's oral agreement. What appears to be a firm promise is a "for instance," a specimen. (The emphatic particle "any" was added by the translator.)

would ask, "If you think there can be extreme cases, what kind of thing do you have in mind?" The defense of Switzerland is the kind of thing Barth has in mind; but he cannot affirm that in a given future particular situation, not yet known, the defense of Switzerland will certainly be commanded by God. He cannot affirm it because by the same principle nothing can be affirmed in advance. Nevertheless, his belief that there can be a *Grenzfall* sometimes is so strong that he feels obliged to give that expectation substance in the form of a hypothetical case.

We face two possibilities. We can seek to define hypothetically the case in which Switzerland would be attacked and the conditions under which war would be commanded, as the *Dogmatics* itself does to justify the application of the extreme case; or we can look at the point in history about which Barth said concretely that war for Swiss independence *was* commanded by God. Then we will have something which it is possible to discuss. We shall turn later to these historical grounds on which Barth could claim that an exception obtained. But for the present we need only observe with regard to the concept of *Grenzfall* what has already been said of the discipline of casuistry as a whole; namely, that the principle that every principle must have an exception is a contradiction in terms; it becomes inconsistent with Barth's own view of revelation as soon as it is affirmed and is not seriously helpful to the structure of Christian ethics.

To exploit the figure of speech suggested by the term *Grenze,* "frontier" or "border," the first meaning of *Grenzfall* as a sign and safeguard of the liberty of God can be seen figuratively as the edge of civilization, beyond which in unmapped territory it is impossible to know under what legislation one lives or how to navigate. At best one can seek to take some fresh bearings on the stars, but that is little help without a map. To apply this with rigor in the field of ethics would be to affirm that the liberty of God is totally unconditioned. We are both ignorant and sinful, so even the maps we had of the homeland are warped. It would be idolatry to make the word "thou shalt not kill" a barrier to God's speaking again, differently, across the frontier which limits our present knowledge of his will. Over and above all human values, over and above all judgments as to the good and the bad, his command is simply free. God is capable of simply commanding something different without providing us with any reasons, without giving us any explanation, without proving it is he speaking, and without proposing to us any alternative.

This would be to understand the sovereignty of God in terms parallel to those of modern pagan existentialism, in which human freedom is understood as being free from God, and accordingly divine freedom is understood as God's being free from any commitment to men. This kind of approach might be reconcilable with the tone of some of Karl Barth's writings in the 1920's, but it would make impossible any kind of Christian dogmatics and thus must be considered unworthy of the Karl Barth of the 1950's. If dogmatics—or for that matter any Christian communication—is possible, we cannot count on situations ever arising in which God would take back what he said in Christ, or give us commands which are not concordant with his revelation of himself in Jesus Christ.[2] When the Christian theologian affirms with the Creeds that "Jesus Christ is the Son of God," he does not feel obliged by his respect for divine sovereignty to say at the same time that there might be extreme cases where this would not be true. Nor does he feel bound to hazard in advance his guess about where those exceptions might be found. In fact, he argues that, precisely because God is free and sovereign, the classical affirmation of the deity of Christ will, when properly understood, apply without exception to all parts of Christian doctrine. It will need constant reformulation and interpretation, but one does not from the inside declare a priori limits to its relevance. Since we have accepted Barth's thesis that ethics is part of dogmatics, we must claim, within the limits of present understanding and subject to correction, the same degree of certainty and universality for ethics as we are accustomed to claiming in Christology. Thus this sort of *Grenzfall* turns out to be not a usable concept within dogmatics or ethics, but rather a limit to the possibility of such a discipline.

[2] "The one Truth of God, in its creative and saving work, has taken the way of the historical Jesus in the midst of all historical reality. Therefore it is here, in the historical reality of Jesus Christ, and indeed in his *humanity*, that we are to discern the one Truth of God at work in and behind all truth." Thomas F. Torrance, *Karl Barth: An Introduction to His Early Theology* (London: SCM Press, 1962), p. 209. Although the heading of this section is "Jesus Christ and Culture," Torrance is not pointing specifically at ethics. Yet what he says would in logic support both our present suggestion that a basically situationist definition of the *Grenzfall* would deny the bindingness of incarnation, and our later impression (below, pp. 70, 112) that the concepts of "justice-state" and "national vocation" are elements of natural or cultural theology not yet fully brought under the judgment of the incarnation.

Second, the *Grenzfall* can be seen as a sign and safeguard of human responsibility. All the ethical thought of Barth is penetrated by what could be called a deep evangelical humanism. In step with some kinds of Christian extentialism, yet more deeply rooted, he sees God in Christ calling man to be more authentically and fully human. Man must take full responsibility for his life, never hiding from God or neighbor behind a rule book. To write the rule book ahead of time is to provide rebellious man a shelter from God's call to freedom and responsibility, and to provide religious man with a tool for self-justification. Thus a too literal interpretation of "thou shalt not kill" not only offends a sovereign God but also dishonors free man, who is then no longer truly himself under the full weight of the decision of the moment. The pacifist himself is not free, and he would put others in bondage to the same laws.

The image here is not that of a desert but of no-man's-land. Across the border there is not an uncharted jungle but rather a conflict of sovereignties coexisting on the same ground with no clear front. The traveler must choose at his own risk whom to follow. He can travel by night with the guerrillas or by day with the pacification forces. He can try to make an uneasy arrangement with both, or to rise above the conflict as a neutral or a mediator, but in every case he must decide for himself, and his decision is valid only for himself.

The third meaning carried by the word *Grenzfall* is its pointing to the finitude, the *Begrenztheit,* of all human values.[3] Life, as a value, is limited. The limits of the value of life are to be found in God's own command, and therefore it can be the case that, in the interest of some other value, the general command not to take life should not apply. Theologically we say this in terms of God's setting a *limit* to each value, but then in the process of decision we discern the limit where one value "collides" with another and we choose the least evil option.

Figuratively, the *Grenze* in this case is a "border" with a known

[3] The first concept of *Grenzfall* portrayed above, as the general rule of exceptions to all general rules, was prepared for in *CD* II/2, although the word was not used there. When the term itself is first introduced it is explained in this third sense. It is used twice in *KD* III/4 with regard to marital ethics (257, 297) but without definition. It is first explained as a concept at the beginning of the discussion of the value of life (388-89), as an implication of the statement that life is always within *limits.* (The translation in *CD* III/4, 342-43, by interchanging freely the terms "limitations," "exception," and "frontier," loses the force of the wordplay.)

country on the other side. We know that if we go across a given frontier we shall be in a given foreign country. We know that in advance, and we can thus affirm in advance that we shall no longer be under the jurisdiction of one government because we will have come under the jurisdiction of another. In ethics there are certain points where human values border on one another and conflict, and we know already that there will therefore be other values to be weighed against the value of human life. Such a value might be the existence of the just state. Human life is *limited,* in the sense that there are other values which at times in the command of God must be preferred to life, namely, when the existence of the just state is endangered. (We must come back later to this contention, in connection with the necessity of defending Switzerland against Hitler. Otherwise to discuss it further would be purely hypothetical.) This sort of understanding of the *Grenzfall* puts us fully in the domain of responsible casuistry and the weighing of value against value, command against command. "Thou shalt not kill" applies, to paraphrase Pascal, on this side of the Pyrenees, not beyond. The divide is the point where another jurisprudence comes into play. If you have an accurate map you need never be lost, and if you ask the gendarme which country you are in you can always know which rules apply in your situation.

The interrelations of the three images should be noted. The sovereignty of God (jungle or desert) and the responsibility of man (guerrilla, no-man's-land) are both clear, theologically derived images of the limits of ethics. They apply in a very clear way. Their application is negative, i.e., to challenge the substance or the relevance or the possibility of an ethical judgment. They do not enable us to say anything positive. The third (Pyrenees), however, is found not in a doctrine of the nature of God or of man but in the objective lay of the land, in the nature of the decision-making process. Here there are no blanks on the map; there is always an answer, but it is not always the same. So what happens in the argumentation of *Church Dogmatics* is that room is first made for the *Grenzfall* on the grounds of sovereignty (jungle) and responsibility (guerrilla). These sources, however, cannot fill the space, for they work only negatively. The space is then filled with the tools of casuistics (Pyrenees), which can make solid affirmations about the future after all.

To explain why we cannot follow Barth at this point, it is not enough to say that the definitions have shifted and the proof is incomplete. We must further observe that the particular *kind* of casuistry which Barth uses heightens the offense against God's sovereignty. First, this is so in logic, because to affirm an exception "limits God" no less (indeed more) than to deny all exceptions. The prediction indicates where the exception will fall. A truly sovereign God could (if his unpredictability is conceived as the test of his sovereignty) just as well command a nuclear war as another kind, aggression just as well as defense. Second, God is bound in practice when the prediction exception justifies the state's institutionalization of its preparation for the exception. This practically excludes the possibility that God might be sovereign enough to be able to make his "normal" will adequate in a given extreme situation, whether by providing for our survival and welfare in ways we had not foreseen, or by giving us the moral capacity to renounce our own existence rather than preserve it unworthily. If God's sovereignty is understood in the royal condescension of Christ rather than in speculation about pure infinity, then crucifixion (the willing abandonment of the genuine values incarnated in the one just Man) and resurrection (the triumph of love over a predictable impossibility) are the modes of the exercise of sovereign authority. From here it would seem to follow in classical Christian thought that God does have power to make relevant and adequate in every situation that which he has already commanded, without being forced by certain situations to "take another line." It is difficult to see how a denial of this would honor God more than the pacifist claim that, if we have once understood God in Jesus Christ, we have no room for predicting exceptions, or even for affirming the possibility of unpredictable exceptions.

The classical just war theory was deeply rooted in the assumptions and the logic of natural theology. This meant that (a) the self (whether the individual or, as his extended ego, the family, the clan, the nation) is a valid locus of ethical value. I have certain duties to my self, and my nation to itself, which are not subordinate or instrumental to my or our duties to others or to God. It also meant that (b) the knowledge needed to make specific choices is derived from "nature" or "things as they are" rather than from new revelation.

At both these points Barth's *Grenzfall* argument is disconcerting.

a. Although the argument began with the appeal to God's sovereignty, in application it reinstates the value of the self. *I* must ultimately decide in faith when *I* must kill to save the values entrusted to *my* nation. There is no hypothetical case suggested of war *against* Switzerland, or of defending the foetus against the mother, or the brigand against his victim. The only exceptions God in his sovereignty seems likely to make happen to coincide with my or our righteous self-interest.

b. Even more striking for the systematic theologian who has read Barth is the concession thus made to natural revelation. The imagery of the divine Word spoken vertically into the given situation is retained, but the substance of the choices to be made is derived from common sense.

If from this analysis we turn back to the treatment of "The Definiteness of the Divine Decision" (*CD* II/2, 661 ff.), we are now better able to ask: Which kind of freedom was Barth writing about there? His concern was to distinguish between the divine command and all ethical idealism. Analyzing the Decalogue and the Sermon on the Mount, he found not generalizations waiting to be applied (or not applied) deductively, but specific demands before which man has only the choice between obedience and disobedience. His adversary was not casuistics; the word "casuistics" does not appear there. What Barth was there concerned to reject is a concept of the ideal law which would still leave men free to decide on their own what the command of God really means. Variety in the specific commands of God is to be expected not because God is jealous of his unpredictability, or because man must make his own decisions, but because God speaks really and bindingly to each concrete decision. The searching reader is even less clear, if he reads *CD* II/2 after III/4 rather than before, about how it is that the concrete man receives these definite commands which are neither identical with the Sermon on the Mount nor derived from moral generalities. Thus if what we bring to *CD* II/2 is our present question about the limits of ethical discourse, we find it reinforcing rather than undermining our search for a responsible casuistic. The very fact that "definiteness" is the theme of the passage forbids making either God's arbitrariness (desert) or man's indeterminateness (guerrilla) the last word. The warning against considering the Bible a "register or arsenal containing all sorts of counsels, directions and commands . . ." (*CD* II/2, 704) is stated not as the major polemic thesis but concessively, with the introduction, "This does not mean, of course . . . ." The main thrust of the immediately preceding section is that "matters are the same here and now [as in the biblical past] and that as and what God commanded and forbade to others, He now commands and forbids to us" (701).

Still another way of understanding the "extreme case" would be to say that human knowledge is finite and that all human statements are open to correction because there might still be further facts to be discovered or further truths to be revealed. Therefore any statement which we make, and this would apply to doctrine as well as to ethics, is made "subject to further notice." This is certainly a very defensible argument. It is certainly necessary for anyone, in any field, making any kind of statement, to maintain at least implicitly the qualification, "This affirmation is valid *as far as I know*." This is the only point at which Barth's introduction to Christian ethics in *CD* II/2 seems to provide anything really parallel to the *Grenzfall*. Here Barth does not speak of the freedom of God in the seemingly existentialist sense which we have seen elsewhere. He does not attempt to argue that, as a matter of principle, every principle must have an exception. He does say, however, that the relevance of our ethical thinking has a limit in the fact that we will never fully know the situation in which ethical decision is to be made. We know, in Christ, the God who speaks to man, but we do not fully know the situation to which he speaks.

The sobering effect of this realization of our limits is not simply a recognition of finitude, as if with better data-gathering methods we might partially escape from it, or as if this inconclusiveness were a flaw in God's working. The point is rather, as the section on "The *Definiteness* of the Divine Command" shows, that, since it pleases God to work and speak within history, to admit the limits of the cross-relevance of our understanding between one point and another is structurally imperative. Everything God says, even if we should understand it perfectly, is said where and when he says it and cannot simply be transposed elsewhere.

This is one argument with which we can fully agree, but we must insist that this impossibility of being absolutely sure of any ethical statement applies just as much to the exceptional case as to the normal case. If it is impossible for finite man to affirm with infinite certainty that God has always forbidden any kind of killing, it is on the same grounds even less possible to affirm that there can be places in which God can and will command killing. Thus this one point at which the explanation of the *Grenzfall* is given a logically valid ground, which would make it a usable term in ethics, is a point which says nothing to the question at hand. The finitude of human knowledge is in itself in no way a ground for assuming that God is going to command participation in war.

We must therefore conclude that the analysis of the concept of the *Grenzfall* itself has given us no new information on the war question. In fact, although we had to ask the question carefully, it would have been a contradiction in Barth's own theory if it had; for then the *Grenzfall* itself would be a new principle, namely, the principle that there must be an exception to every rule. We are driven therefore to conclude that the *Grenzfall* is not a formal concept with validity in the discipline of ethics.[4] It is simply the label which Barth has seen fit to attach to the fact that, in some situations, he considers himself obliged to make a choice which runs against what all the formal concepts of his own ethics would seem to require. Barth has not constructed in the *Grenzfall* a reliable method of theological ethics in which it would be

[4] The first draft of this text had barely been written when this interpretation was confirmed by Prof. Hendrik van Oyen, Barth's Basel colleague in the field of theological ethics, in an article entitled, "Is There an Evangelical Ethic for Extreme Cases?" ("Gibt es eine evangelische Ethik der Grenzfälle?" *Zeitschrift für evangelische Ethik* I/1 [1957], 2 ff.) Van Oyen studies the section "The Protection of Life" as a careful exercise in responsible casuistics, and finds it less than convincing. For each of the hypothetically justified *Grenzfall* cases of justified killing suggested by Barth, van Oyen imagines another possible way out. It can be argued that van Oyen thereby failed to respect fully the hypothetical and not definitely predictive shading of Barth's intent. But if Barth's own colleague could thus imprecisely understand him, does this not demonstrate that the possibility of just this misunderstanding is inherent in Barth's use of terms?

In a somewhat similar way Roger Mehl, one of Barth's most competent and sensitive French interpreters, writing just after the 1956 Franco-British Suez expedition, could consider it an open possibility that that military operation might have been a legitimate *Grenzfall*: "Of course we leave undecided the question whether these objectives, however valid they might be, authorize a *military* operation, and whether we had truly come to that limit-situation where it becomes legitimate to have recourse to arms." ("Remarques sur les Relations de la Foi Chrétienne et la Politique," *Foi et Vie,* LV No. 4 [1957], 309).

Mehl does not propose an affirmative answer; but the very fact that in such a case he can consider the question an open one is an indication of the openness to possible wars which he understands to be Barth's position, and of the casuistic character which he ascribes to the concept of the limiting case.

It is an even more powerful indication that Barth has let himself be misunderstood, that when Mehl "leaves undecided" the question of whether this is a *Grenzfall,* he can go on dealing with the Suez adventure as a hypothetically admissible political option, when for Barth such military recourse would have been categorically excluded *except* as such a case.

possible to found either logically or with relation to the revelation of God in Christ the advocacy of certain deviant ways of acting, such as killing when killing is otherwise forbidden. He has simply found a name for the fact that in certain contexts he is convinced of the necessity of not acting according to the way God seems to have spoken in Christ.

X
The Concrete Case Described Hypothetically

The only way to carry our present discussion further is to go to the study of particular cases. Barth's affirmation that God can in the future command the defense of Switzerland, as he has done in the past, is really the level at which we are forced to converse with him. We must be ready to discuss and study every pertinent case and every argument for such a case which Barth brings forward, and to test those arguments against that revelation which is always the norm of Christian ethics.

This means that we must, because of Barth's own approach to ethics, become almost personal in our analysis. We must come uncomfortably close to passing judgment upon a precise historical situation, even though it is not possible for us to measure fully all the factors involved, or to participate in the process of decision which then went on. Yet this awkwardness is no greater than the awkwardness of Christian theology or of Christian ethics at any point. To repeat: ethics is precisely, according to Barth, a process of checking, by the norms of revelation, those affirmations which people make about the reasons for their decisions. We cannot check the rightness of any decision—God alone is judge (and pacifists, having stood alone for years for the right of the conscientious objector to obey his own convictions, will be the last to condemn an individual for his choice)—but we may check the rightness of any argument brought forth to explain that decision.

In this way, without having any intention of judging whether Barth's decision to defend Switzerland during Hitler's time, by force if need be, was a decision which he made before God, or whether it was right in the sense that it expressed or furthered his communion with God, we must still inquire about his reasons. Indeed, it is Barth's own theology which requires us to ask that we be permitted to see the grounds which he brings forth to explicate that decision. That is the point where the kind of casuistic argument comes back into action which in theory Barth had attempted to declare illegitimate, but without which in practice he is unable to get along.[1]

[1] It is striking how seldom, in all the flood of literature advocating "situation ehics," an operational answer is suggested to the question, "How can one ascertain what God really does say in a given situation, and distinguish between that Word and false guidance?" (This phrasing, with its reference to God's will being known by God's speaking in the situation, is current in Barth and in others whose situationalism has a Protestant-existentialist character. For other kinds of situationists, e.g. Joseph Fletcher, God's speaking is limited to the initial "Love and do the best you can"; God then says nothing more in the situation. The argument of this section applies to both types of situationist logic.) So much effort is expended in attacking outmoded legalisms that little time is left for describing an alternate mode of ethical thought.

This issue is routinely defined (cf. above, p. 14, n. 2) as if the alternatives were rigidity versus flexibility. Yet neither in logic nor biblically are these the options. In logic certainly any right decision must be always both rigid and flexible, i.e., in some sense representing continuity with former commitments and in some sense adapted to the options available in the given time and place. Even the determination to make no basic changes or "never to compromise one's principles" calls for guidance in meeting new situations—for what does it mean in the new situation not to compromise? At the other extreme, even a decision to abandon oneself completely to the passing pressures of the moment would still call for a choice of which pressures to notice. "Shall there be adaptation to the situation?" is thus a meaningless question, to which no really negative answer could conceivably be given. Such slogans as "love is the only absolute" or "do what the situation demands" are not clearly false but merely semantically vacuous, unless undergirded with substantial criteria to help weight the various competing nonabsolute demand claims.

We have said this on grounds of logic; but the New Testament perspective is no different. The apostolic writings affirm clearly that God speaks through his Spirit to given situations in a very real way; they also affirm that there are other spirits, who make other demands also in a real way, and that the way to tell them apart is to compare what they say with the work of Jesus Christ (I Cor. 12; I John 4). Until the advocates

In the study of cases, to use the actual cases in the testing of ethical generalizations does not mean that we stand in moral judgment on the actual decisions as made, or on the persons making them, but that we seek to discern how the process of "testing the spirits" is conceived and carried out. *Church Dogmatics* finally states the definition in a mere half-page of four sentences, whose syntax and substance are so parallel that together they form but one affirmation: "It may well be that in and with the independence of a nation there is entrusted to its people something which, without any claim or pretension, they are commissioned to attest to others, and which they may not therefore surrender" (*CD* III/4, 462). This brief affirmation comes after twelve pages devoted mostly to the rejection of reasons usually given for war, beneath which, however, the undertow of warning had always been discernible that a pro-war

---

of the *Gebot der Stunde,* the Mandate of God to the moment, have explained how they intend to "test the spirits," we must consider their critique of classical casuistry as a form of theological adolescence; valid in what it criticizes, but incapable of finding an alternative that is in the strict sense responsible, i.e. capable of giving an accounting for its decisions before the bar of some authority higher than the self.

We have judged the situationist claim logically and biblically; we could also test it from the practice of those who were using this language about ethics in the 1930's. For over ten years a great number of German Christians, among them very able theologians, set in motion largely by Barth at the historic Barmen Synod, were resisting Hitler. For the last half of this period Hitler was waging an unjust war, of which Barth could say that a soldier defending his country's borders was defending the church of Jesus Christ (this was said first of the Czechs in the famous letter of Barth to Josef Hromádka in September 1938, but applied just as well to the French, Dutch, British, and American Christians later). Yet never did the seeking and resisting of thousands of sincere Christians in a situation as nearly black-and-white as one can imagine lead to their receiving a *Gebot der Stunde,* a Word of God to the situation, which would have told them, as the *hic et nunc* theory requires, to stop participating actively as soldiers and chaplains in this unjust war. To have been conscientious objectors at that time would not have been pacifism but simply respect for the just state, which in this situation was being defended by Germany's national enemies. It would have been not legalism but Christian liberty. Yet since they faced the situation without clear ethical criteria, they received no Word of God to the situation. The one great oppositional effort, that in which Dietrich Bonhoeffer shared, went along with the war, rather than refusing to fight, in the hope of being able to kill Hitler. Barth's judgment on this case of tyrannicide is that it probably was not commanded by God because D. Bonhoeffer and his colleagues failed to bring it off (*CD* III/4, 449). It is not fully sure whether Barth understands this as a failure of conviction, a loss of nerve resulting in inadequate execution (a very dubious criterion when one remembers that for Barth as for Lutherans *Anfechtung,* doubt, is an essential part of belief, the sole safeguard against self-righteousness), or a veto of providence in not letting a risky enterprise succeed. In either case this sample hardly convinces one of the adequacy of the situationist mood. Must one not claim that the only truly evangelical "situation ethics" is one which has sufficient faith in the universal relevance of Jesus' Christ-hood that it dares to judge every situation with the criteria of the New Testament?

statement would be coming. After the four parallel descriptions beginning "It may well be . . . ," the affirmation concludes with two broad statements of ethical method and one specific one:

> "Christian ethics cannot possibly deny that this case may sometimes occur. The divine command itself posits and presents it as a case of extreme urgency."
>
> "I may remark in passing that I myself would see it as such a case if there were any attack on the independence, neutrality and territorial integrity of the Swiss Confederation, and I should speak and act accordingly."

Our concern now is not with the general statements of method. The sentence "Christian ethics cannot possibly deny . . ." is acceptable in one sense, but only in the sense that "Christian ethics cannot possibly affirm" either. "The divine command" is precisely what we are looking for: to drop this resounding phrase in our laps undefined (as was *not* done for the cases of abortion or euthanasia) tells us nothing we can test. So we must turn to the concept that the defense of a nation can be commanded by God when a people stands in a relation to God which would be threatened by the fall of a national state. "It can be that the very existence of the structure of political life within a given nation is something which has been given to that nation in trust by God, which that nation has no right to abandon." Here we have at least two presuppositions which need theological examination. The first is that a "people," in the sense of a nation-state, can stand in a special relation to God and can hold in trust from God certain values, which are to be defended at all cost, or at least at very great cost. The second presupposition is that this people's special relationship to God is dependent upon the continuing existence of the political structure of the state. These presuppositions as Barth states them here are neither debatable nor theological; they are, he seems to say, simply the objective historical fact with which we have to reckon. Yet it is hard to see how it could be claimed that such assumptions are so factual as to be free from the relevance of Christian criticism.

When one submits to the judgment of Scripture the questions, "Can a 'people' be especially related to God?" and "Can the special relationship of the people to God be grounds for preserving at all costs that people's political structure?" the answer is clear. The question of what it means to be God's people and the question of the relation of statehood to the existence of God's people are questions to which Christian revelation speaks. These are not questions of undebatable empirical fact; they are questions of theology. The "definiteness" with which God spoke to his people in Old and New Testament times related most deeply and concretely to experiences of peoplehood under God, and often they involved the issue of how this peoplehood should relate to the structures of nationhood and empire. The Old Testament is the history of a people which did have a special relationship to God and which sought to express that special relationship by justifying its national self-defense. The witness of the Old Testament is that that attempt failed and that God's people's proper self-defense consists in defenseless suffering. What Judaism did not finish learning, Jesus Christ himself confirmed as being the heart of God's way with his people. This would seem to teach that the more closely a people is related to God, the more closely a people is conscious of and faithful to its divine calling, the less the existence of that people can be tied to the political integrity and institutional prosperity of any state structure. The point at which Scripture concedes to the state the least qualified right to exist is when the state is like that of pagan Rome in the time of the apostles. Rome was at its best that kind of a state which precisely does *not* make any claim to a special relationship of its people to God, but simply seeks to keep order.

The argument that it is possible in the plan of God, after Christ and after the breakdown of Jewish national particularism, for any people, anywhere, other than the Christian church, to have any special calling from God, of such weight as to impart to the continued existence or structural autonomy of that nation a value higher than that of the lives which would be lost in preserving it, is a most dubious contention. Such an attitude smacks more of Europe's Christendom tradition and of the sentimental appreciation which some modern Europeans still have for the Holy Roman Empire than of the eschatology of the New Testament.

The biblical attitude toward the specific ministry of God's people is so fundamental that one is triply surprised by Barth's statement here:

a. that it should not have occurred to him that his fourfold affirmation of the concept of the divine mission of a nation should need elucidation;

b. that it should not have struck him that such a taken-for-granted vision of the national mission is a prime example of the same kind of acceptance of extra-biblical value statements which he had elsewhere so consistently condemned;

c. that even if he was resolved to import extra-biblical ideas just this once, he should so easily have picked precisely on anti-biblical ones.

Next, one must ask in what that "special relationship" consists. Is it a result of the fact that a certain percentage of Swiss citizens is baptized? Or of the fact that, in a political analogy to Pauline church order, Swiss women do not vote? Does this mean that only Christian states may justly defend themselves, whereas war would always be wrong for Muslim or Hindu or Marxist states? [2] We would hardly be dealing respectfully with Barth if we took seriously any such hypotheses. But what then can he mean?

Barth had previously ("Near and Distant Neighbours." *CD* III/4, esp. pp. 298 ff.) demolished traditional ideas of the *Volk* as a moral agent or a value in itself.[3] Just what the "relationship to God" is remains ambiguous. If it is nothing more than the fact that the state guarantees the ordered life of the national community, he has not explained in what sense that order is a "relation to God" or why all values are dependent to such an extent on the existence of that *particular* state.

[2] The Dutch theologian A. Th. van Leeuwen (not a pacifist) makes this point especially clear (cf. p. 41, n. 1). If the God to whom a people like Israel has a "special relationship," is one who revealed himself by a crucifixion, it is difficult to see how the "special relationship" can lead to self-defense. Should it not rather lead to suffering servanthood including unmerited death?

J. J. Buskes, in a critique of van Leeuwen's critique, in *Militia Christi* VIII No. 7 (April 4, 1953), claims that van Leeuwen's comparison with Israel is out of place, because Barth (in *KD* III/4, 528 [*CD*, 462]) does not speak of a *special* relationship of "a people" to God. It is true that the word "special" is not used, but there must be something very exceptional (though of course not unique as was the case for Israel) about the relationship of this particular people to God, if (a) it would be lost if the given people's present political integrity were lost; (b) it calls the people to self-defense through war which includes theft, pillage, lying, fornication, and all the rest, whereas in Barth's opinion there may be many cases where a people should, as did Israel in the times of Jeremiah and of Jesus, abandon its state; (c) this people's relation to God is enough closer than that of the aggressor to justify this kind of defense. The language Barth uses is that of religious mission: "something which they are commissioned to attest," "something which must not be betrayed," "more important to them than the preservation of life itself," "thus forbidden by God to renounce."

[3] Even more pointed was Barth's critique of the *Volk* as a locus of moral obligation when it was held by the "German-Christian" movement that by virtue of the "Orders of Creation" or of "Providence" one's nation is an ultimate value.

If, on the other hand, the "relation to God" is more than the possession of a just social order, then both the critique from Covenant history and that of "Near and Distant Neighbours" become applicable.

Here we must keep our critique in proportion. Even if Barth's argument here were convincing and even if it could be claimed that the Swiss people has a special relationship to God that could and would be effectively protected only by military force, the fact remains that the problem facing the world and Christians today is not a threat to the political integrity of Switzerland, but rather the threat of world war. Switzerland has in the recent past kept out of the world's wars, and, even if she should enter into a future war, she would not be its center. This fact in itself does not so much weaken Barth's argument as it demonstrates how nearly pacifist Barth really is, with relation to any real problems confronting the rest of the world. When Barth brings forth this hypothetical argument as to a future attack upon Switzerland, or the historical argument as to a past danger of attack on Switzerland, he has really demonstrated that theologically it is getting more and more impossible to imagine any justification for war waged by any countries larger, or less democratic, or less Christian, than the Helvetic Confederacy. War is possible from now on, according to the logic used here, only for the strictly defensive protection of small Christian democracies. Whatever one might say about the validity of that argument in the case it projects, it is clear that it has little to do with the wars which are today being prepared for and feared and waged all around the globe. Thus by insisting on being called a nonpacifist because he advocated preparedness for Switzerland, Barth has left room for a distorted understanding of his position by people in other countries who face other kinds of wars.

XI
Switzerland's Choice

Our study of the case where war may be commanded, by testing the concept of a nation's special mission, so far has raised more problems and questions than it answered. It has raised new questions about the concept of national mission rather than answering our earlier ones about how one discerns a *Grenzfall.* The only remaining path of investigation is to examine the historic case itself, the final and undebatable fact in Barth's own position and thus the point at which we can understand his deepest motives. His writings and speeches during the Hitler period make clear, clearer than his specifically doctrinal writings, the kind of sentiment in which he justified preparation for the defense of Switzerland whatever the cost. To summarize his arguments at that time is rather simple, for they were single-minded.[1] Hitler was a threat not only

[1] We have already referred to the parallel materials, mostly letters, concerning the duties of French, Dutch, British, and American Christians. Neither this brief summary nor that of Will Herberg (cf. below, p. 119) can do justice to the wealth of pastoral and practical political insights in these writings. They would warrant a separate treatment in a study of

to international order, but to the essence of what a state should be. Hitler's Germany was a state based, as no other state had been in recent history, upon injustice. Faced by the choice of either accepting Hitler's dominion or preparing for military self-defense, Barth concluded that some things are worse than war. Consequently he saw himself obliged by the situation and thus bidden by God to defend the state, in the form of the Swiss state, by force.

This is a form of what has come to be called the "lesser evil" argument. Barth's systematic arguments, his criticism of casuistry, and his concept of the *Grenzfall* really do not in themselves suffice to prove that war should be advocated, but simply leave room for war to be considered necessary on other grounds. It is only here, where his argument is stated in the form of a concrete choice between two evils, that we find Barth at the point where his own reasoning roots.[2] Rather than responding to him here by a simple display of Christian idealism, we must ask what he means by the "lesser evil" argument and whether this argument, which is at the base of all the others, has been dealt with theologically; that is, whether it has been submitted to the criticism which comes from a confrontation with God's revelation of his command to men in Christ.

Under what conditions is such reasoning theologically legitimate, responsible, and defensible? For an argument based on the calculation of probable evils to be taken seriously, we must identify a certain number of formal requisites. These are rooted not in any particular view of

wartime pastoral care; but they are notably lacking in systematic ethical substance. The necessity or inevitability of the war having been decided, its rightness is in these writings a foregone conclusion, henceforth to be presupposed, nor argued.

[2] "There is one price which cannot be paid with a good conscience to avoid this awfulness [i.e., of war] and to keep the peace, . . . namely the wider spread of the rule of a spirit . . . of conscious falsehood, of intentional injustice, of consistent contempt for and violation of men . . . . The rule of this evil spirit is what is still worse than war" (*Eine Schweizer Stimme*, p. 123). Barth does not use the phrase "lesser evil," since he emphasizes that, when necessary, such actions should be carried out with a good conscience. "The more calmly we perceive and concede that we all alike stand under God's judgment in this war, . . . the more cold-bloodedly and energetically will it be waged, for then one . . . will have a good conscience amidst this hard and horrible affair" (*ibid.*, p. 279). So the "lesser evil" is not evil in the sense that one should feel guilty about it. Yet the logic that is at work when the *Grenzfall* of necessary killing is identified is still the "lesser evil" kind of logic. Prof. Barth did not hesitate to use the phrase orally, and agreed with this description when he reviewed in the summer of 1957 an earlier draft of this text.

morality but simply in the requirements of meaningful conversation. The simple statement that one alternative is worse than another is not sufficient. For the argument to be usable in the discipline of ethics it must be used responsibly.

It would of course be possible to deny that the question may properly be put in this way at all. Did not the extended affirmation in *CD* II/2 of the "definiteness of the divine command" lead us to expect some other channel of ethical knowledge than the weighing of available alternatives, and some other content than the inevitable? Is the "lesser-evil" logic then not a misunderstanding of Barth's initial intention? Should not the freedom of God undercut our readiness to acquiesce in the apparently necessary?

What we are attempting here is a "Barthian" critique of Barth's writings on war. It will in effect be our conclusion that this argument, as we find it in the *Grenzfall* exceptions regarding killing, is ultimately inconsistent with, and unworthy of, not only the general affirmations of *CD* II/2 but also the bulk of the argument of III/4. Nonetheless, the treatment of this concrete case is the only terrain where the ultimate case is argued. The Word of God is not a bolt from the blue producing utter subjective certainty disconnected from the weighing of political fact. Only very seldom is it perceived as utter subjective certainty *in* the weighing of the facts.[3] It is not to be identified through any kind of ecclesiastical decision-making process. For each of these interpretations of Barth's intention one could find some basis somewhere in his writings, but they do not reach all the way to his conclusion. The weighing of evils does.

The case of Hitler facing constitutional democracies was of course less ambiguous than that of a battle between two democracies or two to-

[3] Such a criterion of subjective immediacy seemed to be applied to the attempted assassination of Hitler. Whether God has said, "Kill in this case!" (or at least whether one has heard him say it) seemed to be determined by whether one will sacrifice his own life to obey (*see* pp. 59 and 77 above).

Since 1950, however, Barth changed the basis for his judgment on the July 20 case. In *Table Talk* he used three traditional just-war criteria: whether the regime was irredeemably unjust; whether all other recourse has been exhausted; and whether the plotters would be able to govern Germany better after the success of their blow. It is on this third point that Barth disqualifies Bonhoeffer and his colleagues as "dreamers" who "were not clear about what would happen afterwards." Thus again, what seemed at first like an unmediated awareness of the command of God settles back into an evaluation of possibilities.

talitarianisms would be. This perhaps made it less obvious that the moral difference between the two sides needed to be argued, but it does not permit us to dispense with argument.

What would it then mean to sustain responsibly the lesser-evil argument? First of all, what must be chosen is not the *lesser* evil but the *least* evil. If we are given a choice between two possibilities, and if those two possibilities are the only open possibilities, then the less evil of the two is the absolute best that is available and therefore the right choice. It is evil in the sense of pain and imperfection, but it is the right action. It is not sin in the sense of culpable omission or commission. But as soon as it can be shown that there is a third possibility, which by concrete analysis of history is not automatically to be excluded, then the less evil of the first two options may be second best of the three and is by the same logic no longer right.

It is fascinating to observe the simplicity with which Barth always assumes that there are only two possibilities. There is the solution of defense against Hitler with the Swiss army or the solution of unconditional cessation of the country's existence. The simplicity and the lack of concern for possible contradiction with which Barth goes on from this point, without having proved it, would be convincing only if he were sure that all other possibilities had been tried and found impossible; but they have not. His own earlier theoretical argument had been that prior to the *Grenzfall* the church must have exhausted all possible avenues for preaching peace. But in his writings in 1938-45 there was no testing of this requirement.

Our task cannot be to provide new solutions for what Switzerland should have done in 1940. But the historian must point to several possibilities which sometimes are logically and historically open and which are not therefore eliminated a priori on the basis of the historical reasoning which is Barth's criterion. These possibilities have as much theoretical claim to being effective in the long run as the apparently easier military solution.

First there is the claim (which might be contested practically in some cases, but cannot automatically be eliminated from consideration) that there are nonviolent methods of resistance. If there is to be resistance, and if the state which is based upon right and upon justice is to be preserved, it is still not demonstrated to the satisfaction of anyone who is careful about reading his history that nonviolence is not a usable tool. This is not to say that nonviolence as a form of resistance is identical with Christian pacifism or with the love of Jesus Christ, nor that it will *always* work. But until it has been attempted *as a form of resistance,* it is wrong to claim that there are only two alternatives; as long as there are more than two alternatives it is wrong to claim that the military solution is certainly the least evil.[4]

If one takes the long view of history, which this kind of "lesser evil" argument does not generally do, it would be hard to demonstrate that the fate of civilization or the fate of human justice has ever, in a perspective of more than one hundred years, depended upon the political triumph or even the political survival of one state or another. On the short range this may very well appear to be the case, but in the long perspective, which is just as relevant for a pragmatic argument which speaks of weighing evils one against another, it is not at all certain that the winners of wars always gain thereby, or that it would be strategically unthinkable for a nation to maintain its identity by abandoning its political structure without a life-or-death struggle, as Judaism has done during most of its history, as the Gauls did before the Romans, the Gallo-Romans before the Franks, the Danes and Austrians before Hitler, the English before William of Normandy, the Swiss before Napoleon, the Hungarians before the Russians in 1956, and the Czechs in 1968. The most effective defense of Roman civilization against Barbarian invasion in the fourth, fifth, sixth, and seventh centuries was not at those points where there was an attempted military defense of the Empire as a political entity, but at those points where, by submitting to the "barbarbians" on the level of external political sovereignty, the Romans were able to maintain their structure of society, their culture, and their language, and even their local political administration, so that the change in official political control was only at the top. What would have hap-

[4] "He does not even mention the possibility of a non-violent resistance to injustice, a resistance which would plunge its roots into the Gospel and the Apostolic tradition as the Pre-constantinian Church practised it. . . . If he had given attention to this non-violent resistance, he would have found another answer to the problem of the 'exceptional case.' The just-war would then have been simply a war without violence, Gandhi's *satyagraha* type, but on a Christian basis." Hannes de Graaf, "God and War in the Theology of Karl Barth," *Christus Victor* (organ of the International Fellowship of Reconciliation, London), March 1957, p. 6.

pened if strategic surrender had been tried by the Swiss is open to question; but that this method is unthinkable is something that has not yet been proved.[5] The necessity and the feasibility of preserving by war the existing Swiss state has been simply assumed.

Thus before accepting the validity of the argument that war is a lesser evil, we must insist that all other possibilities have been honestly examined. There is no written evidence to show that this was done when Barth decided that war was necessary in 1939 and 1940. Granted that there were few people available who were interested either in showing or in looking for other possibilities, the classic Christian confession remains that "with God all things are possible." If this New Testament claim is at all relevant for ethics (and it would be hard to see why a priori it should be assumed not to be of any relevance at all, just because its tone is pious), then every calculation of a "lesser evil" which presumes to give men the right to disobey conscientiously the major line of God's command in the interest of some proximate good, is open to serious scrutiny. When Karl Barth decided between armed defense and the sacrifice of the just state as the only two possibilities for Switzerland (assuming that Switzerland was Christian),[6] and assuming that Switzerland could preserve its Christianity only by preserving its political structure—did he make that decision in the light of an affirmation of faith that with God all is possible? The lack of any recorded search for a third possibility forbids an affirmative answer. We have no grounds

[5] The dramatic events of October 1956 in Hungary and of August 1968 in Czechoslovakia have brought new refutation of the claim that nonviolent resistance is possible only for Hindus. The violent rebellion of the Hungarians, although extensively planned and powerfully armed, was crushed within days by the repression it called forth. Then a general strike, spontaneous and unplanned, to which the Hungarians resorted after their best forces were destroyed, crippled the Russians and their puppets for months. What could have been accomplished by a well-planned campaign of noncooperation, with leadership and discipline comparable to that consumed by the revolution, which by avoiding the initial violence would have robbed the Russians of their pretext for armed intervention, is incalculable. It is striking how little attention is paid, by those who take for granted the two-choice concept of the lesser evil, to the history and the studies of nonviolent techniques usable for defense (or even, in the Gandhian context, for obtaining rights not previously enjoyed).

[6] Here the term "Christian" is used as shorthand for the further undefined special national vocation or "divine trust" or "relationship to God" which must be defended by war. Barth does not simply identify the Swiss state as Christian, but neither can his language be taken to mean no more than the possession of humane, democratic political order (cf. above, p. 80, n. 2).

for questioning the Christian faith and sincerity of Barth's personal decision; to evaluate personal decisions is, as he says, not the task of ethics. But the reasons with which he explains that decision fall short logically as well as theologically. The whole "lesser evil" argument is in reality an attempt to "tie God down," to deny on the ground of human insight the availability of a saving alternative. Is this not another form precisely of what Barth had forbidden us to attempt in his argument against "general principles"? This is at least what he seems to be saying when he decides on the basis of a short-range view of political history and a two-dimensional analysis of the present political scene that the only two possibilities are total war or total injustice; he denies that God is the source of new possibilities, also for the political order.

For Jesus the apparent options were acceptance of the existing order together with the Pharisees and Sadducees, violent rejection of it with the Zealots, or emigration with the Essenes. Yet Jesus took another path, identical with none of these.

A parallel from the history of dogma may illustrate this point. There came a time when the affirmation "Jesus Christ is the Son of God" was seen to be philosophically impossible. Christ could be a segment of the One God, or he could be a second God, but he could not be God's Son. Christian theology refused to accept this set of alternatives and discovered a third possibility, the doctrine of the Trinity. A similar thing happened soon afterward when a new set of alternatives was posed: Christ can be man or he can be God, but not both. Again Christian theology refused both alternatives and found a new answer, the doctrine of the two natures of Christ. This solution was not available ahead of time; it was worked out only because it had to be, and it had to be only because, in the face of only two possibilities, the church rejected both as inadequate. The solution reached had its weaknesses, but it was better than either of the others. If dogmatics has the freedom, indeed the duty, to insist that there must be in every age a usable way of expressing the Christian message faithfully, and to refuse the alternatives posed by unbelief, then ethics as a part of dogmatics should have the same right.

This consideration is of no help in ascertaining what the third (or the nth) choice might be, nor does it prove (in logic) that that further option will be without violence or without sacrifice of national values. It says only that the burden of proof is still with the advocate of the necessity of war.

The second major logical criterion of the lesser evil is a pragmatic one. What is the likelihood that the line of action which is advocated will produce the promised results or prevent the threatened loss?

Traditional theology has always said with reference to the doctrine of the just war (which Barth here resurrects in another form)[7] that a

[7] A wide stream of speaking and writing in the past twenty years has rejected the concept of "just war" as no longer conceivably applicable to modern warfare. Such rejection of the phrase has been argued not only by pacifists, but by nonpacifists as well. Sometimes the nonpacifists mean that, although war cannot be said always to have been wrong, it can never be right with modern weapons. They then become "practically pacifist" for the present. Others intend to go on preparing for war but recognize that it is not a "just" (i.e. righteous) deed. (Cf. the 1948 Amsterdam WCC assembly declaration: "Even though entering a war may be a Christian's duty . . . modern warfare . . . can never be an act of justice." *The First Assembly of the World Council of Churches,* W. A. Visser 't Hooft, ed. [New York: Harper & Brothers, 1949], report of assembly section IV, "The Church and International Disorder," p. 89.)

This is a most confused line of thought. The historic "just war" doctrine did not mean that a war that met its criteria would be righteous or holy, but only that it would be justifiable. Both "nonpacifist" positions just described are then really applications of the traditional just-war pattern of thought and differ only in their concrete judgment on the justifiability of specific, currently conceivable wars.

Barth does not join in this pointless polemic against a phrase. When he describes past thinking on this subject as "a particular Christian perversion becoming more and more unbearable" (*CD* III/4, 455), he means not the just-war theory as officially held by the moralists (and seldom applied by political decision-makers) but the "post-Constantinian theology of war" (460) with which churches have declared war righteous and good.

Barth does not hesitate to retain the phrase "just war" (462-63, although in some of the occurrences of the phrase in *CD* the German is different). He voices no objections to the detached rationalistic, objective way in which the doctrine is often considered applicable, or to the "natural law" character of the criteria.

Since he accepts the term, he might better have explicitly followed the outline for casuistic sifting of "exceptional cases" which that doctrinal heritage provides. He does not (a striking omission five years after Hiroshima) deal at all with the criteria of "just and appropriate means." With regard to "just authority," it is clear that in his mind this criterion applies negatively to the Hitler regime and affirmatively to Switzerland and the Western democracies, but his only guidance in further identifying a government which may justifiably fight is the concept (462) of a unique divine trust, which is also his only answer to the question of "just cause."

G. J. Heering, "Karl Barth over het Oorlogsproblem," *Vox Theologica,* November 1961, was the first to point out that for all his claim to be more critical of war than the theological tradition, Barth made no serious use of the classic criteria such as just means. Van Leeuwen ("Oorlog als Ultima Ratio," p. 622) sharpens this by reminding us that Barth's description of war emphasized the *everything goes* character of war: "War does in fact mean no more and no less than killing, with neither glory, dignity, nor chivalry, with neither restraint nor consideration in any respect" (*CD* III/4, 453). "To kill effectively, . . . must not those who wage war steal, rob, commit arson, lie, deceive, slander, and . . .

war can be a lesser evil only when it is won. As soon as one loses a war, one must suffer both evils: both the killing and the loss of sovereignty. Certainly, then, the path that has been chosen has not brought the lesser evil. Thus it must be proved, if we are to accept this argument at all, that military defense or readiness for military defense is itself going to be effective—at least that it can argue a preponderant probability of effectiveness. Otherwise it is certainly not the lesser evil. Assuming for the moment that Barth was right that it is better to kill, or to be ready to kill, a certain number of Germans than to have Hitler's state engulf Switzerland, it is immediately obvious that killing the Germans and letting Swiss people nevertheless be killed and Switzerland be engulfed in Hitler's state, then not as an unwilling protectorate but as a conquered enemy, is still less acceptable.

The necessity of providing pragmatic proof for an argument based on intended realism is the test which Barth is attempting to evade by his claim that, curiously enough, it will be the "distinctively Christian note" in the church's message when, after having decided that it is the will of God that Christians fight, the church will make that proclamation unconditionally, regardless of chances and consequences (*CD* III/4, 463). It is startling to see Barth bring back into the argument with considerable emotional power precisely the kind of ethical absolutism and appeal to unconditional value which he was earlier attempting to eliminate.

To state the problem more exactly: It is not fully certain whether the absolutism on which Barth falls back here is that of unconditional subjective certainty which we have observed before as Barth's existentialist undercurrent.[8] "For if the venture is envisaged only in conditions which seem to guarantee success; if there is an eye to the prospects; if the resolve to fight depends on the greater or lesser chances . . . , then obviously no categorical summons to war has been issued either by what has to be defended or by God" (*CD* 463). Whether "a categori-

fornicate?" (454). When Barth thus emphasizes that war is not susceptible of modest, rational control, and further makes a point of its being equally justified if it is hopeless (cf. the "particular Christian note," p. 41 and n. 1), he is evidently not only careless about the discipline of just-war thought, but he rejects the sobriety sought after by its careful limitations. But after all, he is really no more critical of war than the tradition has been. Jacques Ellul, *Violence* (New York: Seabury Press, 1969), p. 7 similarly objects to Barth's reduction of the doctrine to the criterion of last resort.

[8] See above p. 32, n. 2, and p. 67.

cal summons has been issued" seems to be determined partly by "what has to be defended," i.e., by values worth dying for in vain, but partly also by the unqualified subjective quality of the "resolve." Here we touch the existentialist undertone we have noticed before.

If the argument as to when war is commanded is based upon a realistic estimate of concrete available choices and their likely results, as when the Swiss face the choice between falling prey to Hitler with costly resistance, or falling prey to Hitler without resistance, then it is a contradiction for Barth to embellish what began as a pragmatic preference with a new appeal to absolutism in willingness to die for a cause. Dying for a lost cause makes sense only for those who believe in "precepts" and "principles" and "causes." It is stupid and self-righteous for those who believe that ethical choice means getting the best possibility out of a given situation. Here Barth's sentimental criterion as to what would be "distinctively Christian" is a contradiction of his own starting point and especially a contradiction of his argument that the choice to be made here and now, the choice about which we shall then be able to say God wills it so, is a choice made upon our appreciation of the facts of the situation before us and the real possibilities which it offers. It is hard to see how, after starting with such realism as his position demanded at the outset, Barth could ever come to say in effect that precisely those countries which have the least chance of being able to defend themselves effectively, the small Western democracies, are the ones for whom war is most likely to be a commanded thing.[9]

A third criterion for the lesser-evil argument, since it is a pragmatic one, is its willingness to take full responsibility for the consequences. An argument which appeals to "absolutes" is not required, at least not by its own logic, to consider the consequences, since its central loyalty is to something which is not subject to human calculation. It may argue consequences in a subordinate, apologetic way, but its case does not depend on such argument. When, however, in the interest of a more direct freedom to meet the need in the situation and to obey God in the hour when he speaks to the situation, one has denied, as Barth has, the possibility of referring to any such set principles and has preferred to base his argument upon the needs of the hour, then the entire argument

[9] Van Leeuwen ("Oorlog als Ultima Ratio," pp. 629-30) likewise questions the usefulness of criteria for national mission which thus favor small, European, "Christian" states.

stands or falls with the historic reliability of the observations and predictions which are made.

Let us use an American example. Those who in 1939 and 1941 advocated American participation in the war against Hitler have no right to escape their responsibility for the shape of the world which has been the result of the alliances (e.g., with Stalin) and the methods (Hiroshima, "unconditional surrender") which were necessary to win that war. Saying, as some advocates of World War II have said, "We need not take the blame for the results of that war since what we wanted was not the war actually fought, but a different one," is precisely the kind of illusion and evasion of reality for which it is customary to scold the pacifists. The idea that military considerations—such as those which in 1941 required an alliance with Soviet Russia and those which today require alliances of the Western powers with dictatorships in Latin America and Spain and Saigon—could be kept genuinely subordinate to the highest idealistic political aims of war is itself a worse kind of illusion than that of Tolstoy. Especially when one has admitted, as Barth has, that war involves every other sin, and when one is aware of what total war means—when one has realized what it means to say "anything goes"—it is no longer permissible to claim that those who on pragmatic-predictive grounds affirm the necessity of a given war can then disclaim responsibility for the untoward long-range effects of that war, on the grounds of their good original intentions.

The argument that war is a lesser evil, if it be valid, must then involve not only weighing the hypothetical sufferings of a captured Switzerland against the deaths of Swiss and Germans which would be brought about by a war. It must go further and promise that the postwar situation which will thereby be created will be better than the postcrisis situation which would have come into being had there been no war. This kind of political guarantee is far from being as simple as Barth's use of the lesser-evil argument would seem.

Fourth, for an argument that war is a lesser evil to have logical validity, we must know more about the criteria on the basis of which it is to be decided which is more important: the political structure (assuming that it be a just one) or human life. This is not a pragmatic question which is simply given in a historical setting. An ethical, yes, a theological judgment has been made when Barth assumes without argument that the existence of a state dedicated to justice is of greater value than all the lives that it could cost to maintain that state in existence. It is first of all an eschatological statement. It is a statement as to the relative importance of human life and the "powers that be."

The statement often used to render this argument more pointed, that "slavery is worse than death," is an argument which will first have to be submitted to Scripture. That slavery is worse than death, and that military means in the hands of Christians are desirable for the maintenance of the "freedom" of some, are not objective facts; they are not the historical situation which stands unambiguous before us when Hitler knocks at our door, but eminently theological presuppositions. They are value judgments which reflect a particular conception of the relationship of redemption to conservation, of the relationship of the kingdom of God to the kingdom of men, which is open to some considerable question.

This particular "better dead than enslaved" argument raises a host of subproblems. One would be whether the concept of freedom is itself clearly defined, whether one is always either completely free or completely slave, whether national independence and human freedom are always correlated. Since those values which are contingent on the survival of Switzerland are not spelled out, we cannot pursue this issue further. But two other sides of the question do demand attention.

a. It could be argued that war against Hitler in World War II was waged to save the Jews from Hitler. The argument that resistance to Hitler would cost fewer lives than would permitting him to attain his aims, since Hitler's aims involved the extermination of certain classes of people, is a conceivable argument, but it is not Barth's, since the defense of Switzerland, which was the purpose of the war for which he was ready, did not include intrinsically either the defeat of Hitler or the saving of the Jews. Switzerland's armed neutrality may or may not have inconvenienced Hitler more than his attempt to make of Switzerland another Czechoslovakia would have; but in any case Switzerland was defending only Switzerland.[10] The calculation was not of more lives *versus* few lives, but of national independence *versus* lives.

[10] The way in which the fate of Europe's Jews has weighed on the conscience of the West has made it easy for retrospective moralizing to simplify the case for the war by pointing to this one gigantic atrocity as providing all the proof one can want that the Hitler regime was absolutely evil and had to be defeated at all costs. This is to forget that

b. The evils are weighed in this case without regard to the agent. In war it is we who kill, and the evil for which we take responsibility is inflicted by our responsibility on the others. In slavery the immorality of enslaving others is the sin of the tyrant. Thus the argument not only mixes different kinds of evil (death, enslavement) but different agents. It not only tries to measure whether six apples are more than ten pebbles but also whether my apples are more than your pebbles. This becomes painfully visible if we analyze the logical short circuit in Barth's key passage (*CD* 462). Speaking of the people whose relationship to God is bound up with the independence of their state, he says that the values which their state defends may be "more important than saving their lives, and thus also more important than the preservation of the lives of those who unfortunately want to rob them" of those values. What interests us here is not the weighing of lives against values (which is of course specifically casuistic), but the equation hiding behind the words "and thus also." Barth assumes here that if a cause is worth giving one's life for it is "thus also" (*eben damit dann auch*) worth taking other people's lives for (and, incidentally, saving one's own if possible).[11] This self-evident equation of other men's lives with one's own, not in order to give one's own but in order to take the lives of others for a cause one is willing to die for oneself so that one need perhaps not die for it after all, is at best hardly a "specifically Christian note."

---

most of the nations which joined to fight Hitler had first joined to bar the immigration of any significant number of Jews. To save the Jews was not why the war began, and the saving of the Jews was not achieved by the war. When Jewish lives were saved it was by nonmilitary means: by diplomacy, by subterfuge and "underground railroads," by personal risk-taking and by case-by-case appeals to the humaneness of some officials. Far from arresting Hitler's genocidal program, the war if anything gave it a pretext and a good conscience.

[11] A similar substitution takes place between the definition and the application of the concept of *Grenzfall*. When it was first introduced, it was as a limit on one's duty to affirm and defend one's own life. "But since human life is of relative greatness and limited value, its protection may also consist *ultima ratione* in its surrender and sacrifice" (*CD* III/4, 398). The "surrender and sacrifice" would normally be understood by the reader in this context to be one's own. Similarly before (pp. 334-35), Barth had spoken of surrendering life, but not of killing. Yet in the application of the concept it is the life of others which one takes.

XII
The Search for Norms for the State

Barth's justification for war as *ultima ratio* we found to be grounded in the particular mission or function of a given state as bearer or guarantor of certain values which its people have no right to abandon. Switzerland was an example of this, but it did not become clear just why. The next step in the exposition and the testing would then be to seek the criteria by which such a worthy state is to be recognized, so that the *Grenzfall* where it must be defended can be distinguished from the other cases where peace at some cost is preferable. Yet in *Church Dogmatics* we do not find a definiton of the state. To find such a definition we are thus forced to fall back on Barth's earlier writings, without being sure that, had he come in *Church Dogmatics* to deal with the state within the framework of Christian ethics or Christian eschatology, he would have taken exactly the same line as he took during the war.[1]

[1] The two occasional writings which we shall find most helpful were written just before and just after World War II (1938 and 1946). They are available to American readers in

Should he have come to such an exposition, Barth would have needed to find a way to locate the state doctrinally at a new point between the places where Luther and Calvin put it. For Calvin, the state was coterminous with the church, in its membership (thanks to infant baptism) and in its geographic extension—in most reformed churches, in fact, orthodox doctrine has called for Christian statesmen to take initiative in reforming the churches (even though such churches did have, in the synod and the eldership, their own government). This Barth cannot accept. He says very explicitly that the civil community, of which the state is a major expression, and the Christian community, of which the visible church is the expression, are not identical either in their composition or in the norms which they are expected to apply.

On the other hand, Barth refuses above all other things to deal with the state the way Lutheranism sometimes did, making it a second autonomous realm within the divine economy, for all practical purposes subject to no norms except those which it feels to be desirable for the protection of its own existence. Some people could thus convince themselves that they were being good Lutherans when they failed to resist Hitler. Barth had to avoid giving the state that kind of exemption from Christian examination which Lutheranism, if not Luther himself, permitted. It is not clear, therefore, whether or not this new point at which Barth would need to situate the state would have undergirded his own contention that its existence is of such value that it can demand, in line with the redemptive will of God, that the Christian not only take human lives to save it, but also accept theft, lying, fornication, and the rest of what he considered to be a part of war.

One of the most important of Barth's works on the state, *"Rechtfertigung und Recht"* ("Justification and Justice," published in English as

---

the paperback collection edited by Will Herberg (see below n. 2; for additional comment on the accuracy of Herberg's own introductory interpretation, see below, pp. 119 ff.). An additional body of occasional writings on the war from between 1939 and 1945 was printed in the (untranslated) collection *Eine Schweizer Stimme* (1945). The study of these wartime materials has illuminated the total analysis but adds no further theological material.

The above lines were first written "looking ahead" from the place where *Church Dogmatics* had brought the question in Vol. III/4 (1950-51). Barth's return to the topic of the state might have come later in the *Church Dogmatics,* within the treatment of eschatology and history. But in fact the subject does not seem to recur later in the series. *CD* IV/3 does deal with Jesus as Victor and with the mission of the church in the world, but not with the state in either of these contexts. Cf. p. 117 below.

"Church and State"),[2] attempts in line with certain New Testament emphases to situate the state primarily within the context of Christian eschatology. The state is one of (or at least renders visible the demands of) those "powers" which have been subjected to Christ since his resurrection and ascension but which still retain a certain degree of autonomy before God. In "Justification and Justice" Barth defends the essential violence of the state. Its essence is its recourse to force. The state can be brought into submission to Christ; then it has the high calling of a "servant of God" and a special place in the scheme of redemption, although it has not lost completely its capacity to disobey. Its last resort is always the sword, which it does not bear in vain.

In contrast to this position, which would not give the state an absolute value, Barth moves in his *Dogmatics* toward two modifications which give us reason to doubt that we can any longer consider this earlier writing as representative. First, at the strictly exegetical level, he no longer accepts in *CD* III/4 the argument which he had earlier held, and in which other scholars (notably his Basel colleagues K. L. Schmidt and Oscar Cullmann) concurred, that the state is to be understood in the midst of those angelic powers whose submission to Christ is incomplete and indirect. He has abandoned this argument on grounds which, to oversimplify, we may call ontological. Since according to his view evil is not possible although real, Barth is unable to assign any possible existence to "fallen angels."[3] The foundation of the state in eschatology which seems, according to the view just mentioned, to be the Bible's explanation, has thus been abandoned in the interest of a view which suits better certain of Barth's doctrinal interests but no longer answers clearly the question of how we are to find a place for the state within theology. This change in Barth's view can only be described as a concession of the exegete to the systematic theologian; it makes it more difficult for us to see how he would answer our question about the rightness of the state's use of the sword.

The second change which took place in Barth's view of the state between "Justification and Justice" and his argument on war in *CD*

[2] Karl Barth, *Community, State, and Church.* Three Essays, with an Introduction by Will Herberg (Garden City: Doubleday Anchor Books, 1960), pp. 101-48.

[3] *CD* III/3, 349 ff. and 477 ff.: cf. below, p. 125, n. 6.

III/4, is that, whereas in "Justification and Justice" the obligation to use the threat of force defines the state, in *Church Dogmatics* the recourse to force is contrary to the real calling of the state, which should be the work of peace. This change is, to be sure, more in perspective than in content. "Justification and Justice" does not say that the state is devoted exclusively to the use of force, but that is the central problem which is actually dealt with. *Church Dogmatics* does not say that the sword is forbidden to the state but calls it an *opus alienum,* a work foreign to the state's real calling. The two texts are not strictly contradictory, but the accent has shifted.[4]

This change in perspective makes our argument much more difficult. Whether the state is essentially to be seen in its police function or in its welfare function will make considerable difference in the weight of the argument that it is to be defended at great cost and with violence.

Whoever questions Barth's insistence that there can be a time and place, and that Switzerland in 1940 was at such a time and place, where war is commanded by God, is therefore placed before the problem of finding where Barth's argument starts. We began with his statement that God is free to command men in a way which does not (apparently) correspond to his earlier command, so that the pacifist is being unfair to God if he denies him this freedom. But when we ask how we can know that it is God who is speaking to command war and not some other god or idol, the only reference we are given is the concrete historical situation, in which a justice-state must be saved. Thus we look for the definition of the justice-state, only to find that the state for whose sake war is justifiable in the extreme case has no unequivocal place within Barth's theology. That there is and must be a state, that a Christian may ask the state to be just, and how the Christian should ask the state to be just, Barth has discussed several times and in several ways.[5]

[4] "Barth's conclusion [in "Justification and Justice"] is the same as in his ethics, but the accent is just the opposite. In this pamphlet not war but the refusal to serve the state functions as the *ultima ratio.*" (Van Leeuwen, "Oorlog als Ultima Ratio," p. 628.)

[5] Although the distinction between "just state" and "justice-state" remains intact, only the latter term is meant here. Positive righteousness can be attributed to no state, but the justice-state commits itself to a standard beyond selfishness or arbitrariness.

The shift in Barth's language could also be formulated thus: In "Justification and Justice," as in all classical Protestant teaching on the state, the normal, essential function of

But why the existence of a justice-state is such a fundamental value that, once it is at stake, a given state must be defended at almost any cost, has never been spelled out. One explanation might have been to assume that the nature and authority of the state was to be dealt with later in *Church Dogmatics,* perhaps within Eschatology (which would fit with the argument of "Justification and Justice"). But this kind of advance cross-reference, building an argument on a foundation which has not been laid, is not typical of Barth. If he was not ready to found the state positively in the order of creation he should perhaps not have dealt with war in Volume III/4.

Those theologians who have learned from Barth that there is no point in the whole realm of human behavior and discourse where theology is irrelevant will thus be startled to find that Barth's argument for war boils down ultimately to the statement that here is a point where we do not start from theology, but simply with the problem of survival. Switzerland must survive; it would be worse if she did not.

Yet what does Christ say about survival? Here it is the pacifist who begins with a theological position. The cross of Jesus Christ is for the New Testament the normative answer to the problems of survival for the individual as well as for God's people. Until we see more clearly how Barth grounds positively the importance of the state as over against the Christian duty of loving and sacrificial service, and over against the cost of another war in killing, lying, burning, pillaging, and raping, we are incapable of knowing on what grounds he wishes to be taken seriously. Barth's statement in one of his wartime writings, "that 'no' to Swiss defense would be a 'no' to the State as such," is still no help with the same two problems. First of all, how can the "state as such," precisely in the exercise of its destructive *opus alienum,* become itself worthy of being defended at any cost in human lives, social virtues, and cultural values, when previously (cf. above, p. 39) its basic justification was as instrumental to other ends beyond itself, and especially to make room for the redemptive work of the church? Second, has another way of saying "yes" to the Swiss state, or to the state as such, been sought? We

the state is the use of the sword, and peace is the ultimate goal, hardly reachable in this life. But in the ethics of *KD* III/4, peace is the present possibility and duty for government, and war can become justifiable only at the edge (*Grenze*) where the peace has failed to be just.

ask this double question, not to stand in personal judgment on Barth's wartime position, but to show at what points these wartime writings fail to make clear just what his position was, or on what grounds he believes his Christian brothers should share it.

After the attempt to ground the state in eschatology, which was made in "Justification and Justice" and later partially modified, Barth made another attempt to describe the relation between church and state in his essay, "The Christian Community and the Civil Community."[6] Does its argument provide a substitute for the grounding of the state in eschatology which Barth had set up in "Justification and Justice" and then abandoned in Volume III/4?

Barth does not seek explicitly to answer this question. This essay simply assumes that the state is present and addresses itself to the problem of the norms which the church or the Christian observer of politics may apply to the state.

It is significant that there is hardly anything controversial in the entire argument. Barth simply tells us that the "good" of the civil community is analogous to the "good" of the Christian community. Since the church is a brotherhood, some analogy to brotherhood should exist in civil community. Since the church is based upon the communication of the Word of God, something like the possibility of communication, which is to say free speech, should exist in the civil community. This method is logically quite possible when one agrees with the application being made. Most of the sample social goals projected by Barth in "Christian Community and Civil Community" can count on wide acceptance from modern democratic Westerners. It is quite possible logically to use analogy for illustrating, reinforcing, and demonstrating that which we consider desirable. But to *prove* anything, i.e., to provide a ground for guidance and clarification within a context of disagreement, the method of analogy is useless.

If anything, this writing of Barth's demonstrates the weakness of his earlier argument for the possibility of war. The very structure of this essay presupposes and explicates a denial that a state or civil community as such can be a self-aware moral agent so as to stand immediately before God as having from him a trust, or as being commanded by God

[6] Karl Barth, *Community, State and Church.* Three Essays, pp. 149-89.

to defend itself. The tone of his discussion of the possibility of war in the *Church Dogmatics* had given the impression that Barth was thinking of Christian ethics as directly relevant to the state. But here in the study of the two communities he recognizes very clearly that "Christian ethics for the civil community" would in a direct sense be a contradiction in terms. The very clear distinction between the two communities is in fact the theological innovation for which the essay is chiefly important, and the presupposition of all its further argument.[7] This text thus leaves us doubting even more than before his presupposition that a national "people" as such can be a moral agent, be responsible or be called by God to defend political independence at the price of other values.

Barth claims that by analogy with the Christian community we may draw certain general lines as to what we may expect or ask of the civil community, but he does not include national self-defense. This is striking since one of his clearest contributions to social ethics in the preceding twenty years had been his advocacy of preparedness for war against Hitler. His silence at this point would seem to constitute a tacit admission that, if guides for action in the civil community are to be drawn from analogous characteristics of the church, we look in vain in the church for an analogy to military defense. The church has often enough in the past attempted to defend herself in the form of her institutional structures. She has often enough said that any means necessary for the defense of these institutional structures is justified because those structures are themselves that which God has entrusted to the church. Yet those arguments of the churches within Christian history are the kind of thing which Barth very clearly sees to be bad theology. He cannot argue *for the church* that she should defend her institutional integrity by whatever means may come to be necessary. Therefore he has no grounds for concluding that the state can also be called by analogy to give its institutional status that degree of support which will permit war on its behalf.[8]

[7] This is not to deny that the state in some ultimate sense stands already under the moral judgment of Christ's lordship. This is what Barth here finds a new way to affirm. But that judgment must be modulated by the recognition that the civil community cannot derive its ethical thought from a common confession of that lordship; therefore even the Christians in that larger community, when they derive their social-ethical witness from their own confession, must reformulate it analogically.

[8] We have dealt here with the logic of analogy the way it seems *prima facie* to be presented, as an approach claiming somehow earnestly to be "right" and testable by the cate-

This unclarity about the nature, criteria, and value claims of the justice of the state permits Barth to avoid coming to grips with the distinction between the police and war. The state which defends itself, Barth says, is defending its capacity to maintain internal order. Thus its defensive action in war is of the same moral quality as the force used by the policemen. Many pacifists would agree with Barth that in extreme cases (abortion, euthanasia) the maintenance of an absolute refusal to take life may be impossible. They will, however, have some difficulty in reading with a straight face Barth's attempt (in *CD* III/4, 399) to use the church discipline of the New Testament, when Ananias and Sapphira dropped dead before Peter's words, in order to open a loophole in the prohibition of killing. Some will go further and admit that the police function within society, whether exercised within the structure of the state (stopping a criminal) or without (self-defense, stopping a tyrant), may be justified. Yet this has nothing to do with war. War differs qualitatively from the police function and even from tyrannicide. Formally it differs in the absence of superior legislative and judicial control and in the fact that it kills without any discrimination between innocent and guilty. That the difference in degree and in concrete horror, and in the creation of further disorder and tension, is incomparably more than a formal matter, needs no elaboration in our day.

gory of "proof." This is the way it must be dealt with if we are asking all along the way for the grounds from which an imperative for war can be derived. But it might be that the individual samples of analogy-type thought are not meant so seriously. There is sometimes a whimsicality or "humor" (his word—note below, p. 128) about Barth's theologizing, in which "what if we tried saying it this way . . . ?" does not ask to be tested rigorously, but suffices to make its point by locating an option. Perhaps the point that the Christian community and the civil community need different modes of ethical discourse is valid apart from the persuasiveness of the particular specimens. Cf. below, p. 126, on the rigidity with which Will Herberg reads Barth here.

XIII
Historical Realism

A quite different arena must now be examined in an attempt to understand and to speak to the Barthian position. Is the position which Barth advocates in place of pacifism historically realistic, and does it correspond to real possibilities more than does pacifism? This is still within the bounds of the "internal criticism" to which we limit ourselves, since political realism is one of Barth's criteria.

First there is the question of balance. Let us grant for the moment that Barth is correct in saying that although pacifism is almost right, there remains an extreme possible case where the pacifist will be wrong. Is it proportionate; does it correspond to his own statements of intent, when Barth uses almost as much space in defending, defining, and demonstrating the necessity of the extreme case as he does in drawing clearly the main line of his arguments? We have said—with no fear of contradiction from anyone who has really read Barth—that he stands nearer to pacifism than any other major theologian within the European Protestant tradition in modern times[1]; yet we can say this only because we have read his works with the intention of finding what he considers basic. For one who hears about Barth secondhand from his students, or for the reader who skims this one section of his dogmatics asking which position he is taking with regard to the pacifist issue, it will appear that Barth condemns pacifism. In reality, however, he condemns much more clearly every other answer to the question. Although they are "very near to the Kingdom," pacifists have missed the whole point, and the good conscience of the typical Swiss soldier-citizen still need not be troubled.[2]

When this passage in the *Church Dogmatics* was presented in the lecture hall in the spring of 1951, there was no student in that auditorium who avoided the feeling that what had gone on that day was not really the affirmation that pacifists are almost infinitely right, but much more a process of damning them roundly with back-handed praise. Thus it can come about that an argument which, as far as real theological content and intent are concerned, is really a kind of pacifism, can be understood in a wider theological and nontheological world as being just the contrary. What Barth really says but does not say loudly and does not state as impressively as he does the doctrine of the *Grenzfall,* is that in most cases, in most wars, and before most threats of war, the normal reaction of the church should be rejection of war, even to the willingness to sacrifice certain state structures, and the willingness to teach all Chris-

[1] It should be remembered that the relative pacifism of *CD* III/4 in 1950 was based on preatomic reasoning. There is only one allusion to atomic weapons (*CD* 453) and it adds nothing to the argument, as he himself later (cf. below, p. 117, n. 7) said it might have. Only in the 1950's was his relative pacifism undergirded with his "neutralist" stance on the cold war, and only about 1958 did it come to focus on atomic rearmament. It is thus all the more striking that his position was taken before his encounter with the reasons which have since led many to be more critical of war, namely the magnitude of the newer weapons and the tendency for militarism to be allied with political reaction.

[2] An index of this effect was the immediate translation and separate printing (December 1951, just six months from the appearance of the German original) of just the section of *CD* III/4 on war, in the Geneva pamphlet series *Cahiers du Renouveau* ("La Guerre et la Paix," Labor et Fides, Geneva). This came as an answer just three months after a pamphlet in the same series, "L'Église, l'Armee at l'Objection de Conscience," in which, for the first time since World War II, the conscientious objector position was taken by a Swiss young man of unimpeachable Reformed theological fidelity and with an excellent previous military record. What purports to be and is literally an unprecedentedly critical opening of the war question could immediately serve to soothe the consciences of a generation of students in the University of Geneva.

Other examples of the same effect may be seen in the use of this passage by Roger Mehl (p. 73, n. 4 above) and by German politicians (p. 117, n. 7 below).

tians that such is the path of faithfulness. The normal situation for the church in most places, in the case of many wars in the past and presumably most conceivable wars in the future, should have been and should be a collective, situational conscientious objection. That is the true Barthian position, but it is not what the superficial reader of *Church Dogmatics* remembers. Barth's position of 1950 would mean that German Christians during the time of Hitler should have been conscientious objectors as a body, and that concerned German Christians in 1960 and 1970 should, on the whole, tend to be conscientious objectors.

We must therefore frankly ask whether the way Barth states his rejection of "pacifism," and the amount of space and the wealth of argument he applies to the demonstration that pacifism is in error because it is absolute, are commensurate with the relative importance of the dangers of Christian conformism and lethargy which, far more than pacifism, stand the chance of leading the world and the Christians into the next war and leaving moral thought in self-justifying bondage.

Since the writing of *KD* III/4, Barth's explicitly stated position moved further in the same direction. Both the ethical interpretation of the meaning of sanctification (*KD* IV/2) and his participation in the efforts of churchmen to oppose the rearmament of West Germany and its incorporation in NATO led Barth to still stronger "practically pacifist" statements.[3] Yet this change remains only relative; it does not overcome the discrepancy between Barth's sweeping critique of past wars and motives for war and the room he feels obliged in principle to leave for future war.

Next, if we are to deal with the realm of historical reality, we must ask whether Barth is not himself being utopian when after having

[3] See below, pp. 133 ff. In a conference of Protestant prison chaplains in 1960, Prof. Barth reinforced his earlier criticism of the death penalty on the grounds that it is a kind of "expiation" which is out of order after the death of Christ. According to the report, "Even in the case of treason in time of war the death penalty is not possible." Prof. Barth at this point expressly retracted his statement on the subject in *Kirchliche Dogmatik* (III/4, 512-13), in which he had left open the possibility of capital punishment in this one case, as he no longer would in 1960. Then he had let himself be too strongly impressed by the situation of Switzerland in World War II. "It is never good for a theologian to think from within the situation!"—more precisely paraphrased, "to take the situation as one's point of departure": *"von der Situation her denken"* (*Junge Kirche,* XXI, August 10, 1960, 407).

This statement says something whose relevance to discussion of Barth's wartime writings reaches well beyond the death penalty issue: namely the retraction of the *Grenzfall* concept; now there is one form of killing for which there is no *Grenzfall* left open.

said that war, even when necessary, is always an *opus alienum,* an activity foreign to the real nature of the state, he then goes on to agree that the state may justifiably not only defend itself but also may plan for its defense and invest an enormous share of its material resources and still more of its human resources in that preparation. Even if the justified war is thought of as the extreme exception, to prepare for war demands a solid institution. Barth advocates general conscription (*CD* 466) and argues that the conscientious objector, who in his commitment to the *opus proprium* of the state seeks to withdraw from the institutionalized preparation for the extreme exception, has the burden of the proof and should not expect any legal recognition, but should rather expect to pay the penalties of the law (Switzerland in 1950 made no legal provision for conscientious objection; only in the 1960's did the Swiss churches even begin to ask for such). Is it realistic, in terms of social psychology and in the light of the experience of highly armed nations, and is it straightforward use of language to retain such phrases as *ultima ratio* and *opus alienum* when readiness for war is thus organized? [4] Or, if modern states are spending in many cases over half their budgets on an activity which is foreign to their real nature, then must the Christian not again ask how such a state can be the "justice-state" which is worth defending? It is difficult, at any rate, to see how Barth can deny that military violence is the normal function of the state and yet at the same time maintain for the state the right not only to prepare that violence but to make it a major concern, and to make it so normal a major concern that the conscientious objector should be a rare exception.

Here we see the practical import of the confusion, already described formally, of varied concepts of the *Grenzfall.* On one hand there is the "double negative" or "desert" sense; the *Grenzfall* means that one cannot with mathematical certainty deny that a situation will ever arise in

[4] "Does not Barth lack a sense of reality when he speaks of war as if it were an *opus alienum* of the State? Is Barth unaware of today's military budgets? . . . Barth is constantly assuming that the states 'possess' armies. Does he not see that it is the armies that possess the states?" (Hannes de Graaf, "God and War in the Theology of Karl Barth," *Christus Victor,* March 1957. De Graaf's analysis was adapted and expanded by Jean-Michel Hornus, "Dieu et la Guerre," in *Christianisme Social,* November 1955, pp. 580 ff.). Heering (*Karl Barth over het Oorlogsproblem*) also challenged Barth's realism as to how governments really make decisions.

which given ethical principles will be inadequate. In this form the concept may be useful, but on the condition that it be held to this meaning. On the other hand, there is its use (Pyrenees) to designate an exceptional case which can be described in advance and for which plans must be made. In this casuistic form, the concept has not been grounded by Barth; yet he uses it this way when he assigns to the state the duty of preparing for war, as becomes especially visible when he speaks of conscientious objection. Can one prepare at great length for an *ultima ratio?*[5] Does the freedom thus given to the state differ significantly from the *carte blanche* which Barth does not want to give the state? Does saying that the state's real purpose (*opus proprium*) is peace and not war retain any realistic meaning in the face of the budgets and the institutional momentum of the modern military apparatus? What remains of the claim that war is not the state's real task (*opus alienum*) when we are told that conscientious objectors should accept as normal that they be treated as criminals?

If we are to take seriously Barth's earlier strictures on war in general, to say that the state should be constantly prepared for war is like saying that an honest man should always be prepared for lying or a faithful husband for divorce; it confuses an extreme eventuality with normality, thus demonstrating the inadequacy of the *Grenzfall* as a tool for straight thinking.

A third point at which Barth falls short of his own demands of realism occurs when he describes (*CD* III/4, 463-64) the church which will speak faithfully to the state. This church, which he describes at the end of his argument, should speak to the state in favor of peace, in favor of justice and order within its borders, and in favor of righteousness beyond them. When the church has said clearly to the state as long as

[5] "How can one prepare for an *ultima ratio* without precisely annulling its ultimate character?" (Van Leeuwen, p. 628). If one is thus to argue that government may make long-range institutional preparations for an action which can be justified only very exceptionally by a Word of God to a given situation, then the least we must ask for is an equally firm institutionalisation, both in the state and in the church (which is supposed to know about the Word of God), of the safeguards against the exception's being declared illegitimately.

When the creation of a costly and powerful political institution for the only potentially permissible war is accepted, it is hardly still true to say (pp. 38-39 above, *CD* III/4, 454) that one views killing in war as even less admissible than euthanasia, suicide, and tyrannicide. For those *Grenzfall* possibilities no institution is approved of.

possible that war is forbidden, then this church and only this church, having so spoken, will also be ready and will know just when the time has come to say to the state, "Now war is the will of God." Our question is very simple: Does this church exist? Is the Swiss Reformed Church Federation an organization capable of speaking to the state with this degree of clarity, of examining and understanding situations with this degree of certainty, of making her voice heard at exactly the right time to say now "peace" and now "war" in such a way that both church members and politicians can count on it? Has there ever existed a nonpacifist church capable of advising a people to sacrifice their freedom? Is it realistic to think that the churches which for generations, yea for centuries, have been saying to the state that war *can be* just and that in line with that conceivable possibility of justice that state may still prepare war, will be seriously listened to by the state if and when, once the landslide has begun, they say, "But not this time"? Does it correspond to anything which can happen in the visible church, when Barth gives us the image of a church which in full clarity and full freedom before the will of God says clearly to her members and to the state, "This war is wrong; now all of us shall be objectors," all the while retaining the freedom to say later, "Now war is right"? Such an assumption, as concerns either the church's capacity to speak or the state's capacity to hear, would seem just as unrealistic as Tolstoyan pacifism.

Barth can answer that he does not expect the Swiss state church to speak as the church, and that in the political realm individuals will always speak for the church. Often, in fact, the organized church will refuse to stand behind those courageous individuals who speak in God's name to politics.[6] Church authorities may even disavow that message (as was the case for Martin Niemöller's opposition to German rearmament, which Barth cites in this connection).

To evaluate this argument would mean going beyond the limits of internal criticism. To systematize it and unroll its assumptions, accepting as normal that the existing organized church does not speak corporately God's Word to the world, would represent a new form of the Reformation doctrine that the true church is invisible, i.e., does not coincide with

[6] "Political Decisions in the Unity of the Faith," in *Against the Stream; Shorter Post-War Writings, 1946-1952* (New York: Philosophical Library, 1954), pp. 147 ff. (German original 1952).

the organized church, so that we may not ask of the organized church what the New Testament asks of the true church. What this distinction means theologically we do not ask here. We might be permitted to doubt that it fits with everything else Barth says about church order (*CD* IV/3) or with the claims of the 1934 Barmen Confession. Suffice it to note that realistically it heightens the difficulty which the state will have in hearing and taking seriously the warnings which the church (which church?) pronounces against a too hasty entry into the war for the preparation of which Barth has given his conditional approval.

Our questioning about realism leads us back to theology. Barth assumes that democracy is qualitatively different from other forms of government. He admits very clearly that the democratic state is something about which the New Testament says nothing. Although the New Testament spoke of church and state as being, if not antagonistic, at least basically different, so that the Christian had no "responsibility" in the modern sense of the word, Barth argues that the novelty of democracy has effected a change in the role of the Christian. Therefore the New Testament really stands to be corrected or, better, "extended," as he says toward the end of "Justification and Justice." We must add to the New Testament view of the state the new fact that democracy is a product of Christianity, or at least that its development is consonant with Christian concerns, and that democratic responsibility is not something to be argued about, but to be welcomed.

This theme belongs not with Christian theology but with Voltaire and the French encyclopedists. The Christian realist will be well able to argue that democracy is better than other forms of government, but he can so argue precisely because he will measure democracy by the same standards as other forms of government. The fact that certain agents (often not the most important ones) of the state are chosen by relatively democratic procedures does not modify the fact that the state is still defined by its claim to the use of violence for the maintenance of order. This is not at all changed by the fact that some, half (as in Switzerland), or even all citizens have the right to vote. That the vote really changes *everything* is a belief that can be maintained only by a romantic whose political ideals were formed before the French Revolution.

Realistically speaking, democracy in its various forms is no more than a better and less overtly violent way of administering human justice. It is preferable to many other kinds of human violence, but that preference cannot be absolute, and especially it cannot be exploited theologically in such a way as to make irrelevant what the New Testament says about the church's attitude to the state.[7] If the difference between democracy in the "liberal" sense and democracy in the Marxist sense, or between democracy in the Swiss sense and democracy in the French sense, or between democracy in the Jacksonian sense and democracy in the Jeffersonian sense is only a matter of degree, then there is no way to avoid the conclusion that the difference between any kind of democracy and any other kind of stable government is also simply a matter of degree, not fundamentally altering the state's functions and sanctions. This makes it still harder to see how saving the specific political structure of the Swiss state, the Dutch state, or the American state can be a value of such clear worth that it takes precedence over the command to love our enemies and over the death of Christ.

[7] Both in *CD* (III/4, 465) and in "Justification and Justice," Barth makes it clear that his approval of democracy is theologically based. There is no intention simply to borrow it from its modern advocates. Yet in neither place is this affirmation supported by argument or by encounter with the data of political science. Barth's clarity later in counseling Christians in Eastern Europe to work willingly within their less democratic societies demonstrates that his preference for democracy is not intended to be doctrinaire.

XIV
Summary

Our summary criticism may be limited to those elements of Karl Barth's argument which seem inconsistent with Barth's own contribution to theology. We began by intending to present to Barth only those criticisms which would be relevant within the framework of his own thinking; we are forced to conclude that his position as regards war is unworthy of some of the insights which are his own specific contribution to the history of theology in the last half century.

One of the things which theologians have learned from Barth, in his critique of all philosophies of religion and all theologies which did not start with revelation, is to respond with a great deal of suspicion when presented with a timeless truth which can be abstracted from the concrete work of Christ. The theologian will be wary of importing philosophical, rational criteria of truth from somewhere other than salvation history. Yet in his discussion of the problem of war, this is precisely what Barth does.

First he does this when he gives us "respect for life" as the equivalent of what it means when God says, "Thou shalt not kill," or when God commands, "Love thy neighbor as thyself," or when Christ commands, "Take up thy cross and follow me." His doctrine of "respect for life" clearly does not give to this term the abstract meaning which it had when Albert Schweitzer coined it, and yet Barth uses the slogan at critical points in a similar way. When he argues that "Thou shalt not kill" means really "Thou shalt respect life" and then "Thou shalt sometimes kill out of respect for life," Barth has really boiled down to a general principle the command of God as stated in the Old Testament or in the form of Christ's cross.[1] Having reduced the command of God to a principle of respect for life, he then has found the point at which two lives seem to be threatening each other, where respect for the principle requires acting in a different way.

The same kind of thing happens at a later point of his argument where Barth treats as a solid value the state committed to justice. "Justice" and the possibility of a state's or a people's being committed to justice in this unqualified degree are concepts which sound, to anyone who has learned theology from Barth, like voices from another sphere. We may well see, in the life of Christ, or in the way which the sovereignty of Christ calls the state to be a servant of God, objective criteria for judging the relative rightness of this or that state. In judging the relative rightness or wrongness of this or that war, "justice" may be a useful concept. But Barth is simply giving us in a new form the dedi-

[1] Our objection here is not to the distinction between "murder" and "killing," which can be supported linguistically and culturally in the interpretation of the Decalogue (though it should not be assumed that thereby it is settled that in the proper Christian, theological-ethical use of the Decalogue only "murder" is prohibited: cf. Jean Lasserre, *War and the Gospel,* trans. by Oliver Coburn [Scottdale, Pa.: Herald Press, 1962], 169 ff.): What we question is the quasi-mathematical logic, which moves from "do not kill" to "respect life" to "do kill out of respect for life" on the quasi-mathematical axiom that quantities equal to a third quantity are equal to one another. This can be done with "z equals y" and "y equals z," because "y" is the same in both. But does the abstract "respect life" have the same meaning in both imperatives? Barth himself borrows from Bonhoeffer a pointed critique of this logic whereby a child reinterprets his father's command "go to bed" as meaning "go out to play," by equating both with "I don't want you to be tired" (*CD* IV/2, 541, from Bonhoeffer's *Cost of Discipleship,* trans. by R. H. Fuller and Irmgard Booth, 2nd ed. [New York: The Macmillan Co., 1959], p. 71). Such a quasi-equation is not only a logical flaw, in that sentences cannot be handled with such algebraically univocal meaning; it is also a moral fault, for if the child receiving the command reserves such freedom to redefine it, there can never be for him a really binding, unredefinable word of command.

cation to "justice" which occidental civilization has received not from Christ and not even from the Old Testament, but from Rome.

The point at which Barth is most completely "non-Barthian" is the point at which, when we ask him what it means for God to speak here and now, he presents us not with the Word of God spoken to the situation, but with the bare situation. Barth has told the pacifists that they are sinning against God's freedom by denying to God the possibility that he might command war. The pacifists can answer that if God commands Karl Barth to go to war he should certainly obey, but what they have not yet seen is that this was truly a command of God.[2] When the reader looks for the identification of God's commandment, Barth brings forth in the last analysis not a word which was spoken through him as if by a prophet in the Old Testament sense, not a mystical intuition or conscientious conviction of divine leading, not a clear ethical value judgment, not a revelatory vision or audition, not an interpretation of Scripture, but simply a political situation in which he saw nothing else for Switzerland to do. The pacifist will have, or at least should have, great sympathy for the difficulties of Switzerland's position in 1939 and the years which followed, but the Christian theologian can never permit this kind of shifting of concepts to take place. When Barth spoke first of the freedom of God to reveal himself in a way which would appear to contradict the commandment "Thou shalt not kill," he was speaking of the freedom of God. When, however, we ask him for the case in which God has spoken, we are confronted with the freedom of Switzerland. We move without being warned out of the field of theology when, having asked how we may know when God has commanded war, and how we may distinguish between his command and someone else's, the only answer we receive is, "What else is there to do?"

[2] In what might be the first book-length analysis of Barth's ethics, Joseph van Dijk, O.P., comes at the end to just this point (*Die Grundlegung der Ethik in der Theologie Karl Barths* [München; Manz Verlag, 1966], pp. 249 ff.). What *is* the Word or Command to the situation? On the one hand there is a simple "biblicism" which would provide grounds for extensive ethical teaching, such as the writing of volumes of dogmatics, but without clarity about the rules which it should operate. On the other stands the unqualified sovereignty of God, who speaks only when and as he pleases, before whom all our efforts to understand and teach are worse than useless, and the most responsible expression of faith would be agnosticism. Neither of these positions, taken alone, would be true to Barth. But how can we take them together?

Various pacifists would respond in various ways to the question, "What would you do?" Some would argue that nonviolent techniques of resistance would have at least as much chance of success in defending what must really be defended as would military means. Others would declare the question itself to be an illegitimate intrusion of selfishness or pragmatism or doubt or natural theology; Jesus did not tell the Jewish nationalists, when he refused to let them make him their king, what he would do in their place to achieve their goals with less bloodshed; he called them to follow him in the renunciation of these goals. Still others would grant to the non-Christian state the freedom to defend itself, but without conceding that the Christian is called to share in that expression of self-affirmation. It is not our task here to discuss whether any one of these answers is valid, consistent, and reconcilable with the others. The facility with which, in Barth's reasoning, the passage is made from this rhetorical question to one particular answer is theologically not justifiable, whatever other answers there might be.

We may restate the question in terms of the traditional language of respectful controversy. Barth's argument seems to displace illegitimately the "burden of the proof." He who argues that war is never concordant with the will of God is challenged by Barth to bring the proof for the hundredth case, even after Barth has admitted that in ninety-nine cases out of one hundred pacifism is right. Logically it would be much more normal for the person who has argued as a matter of principle that there can be no hundred-percent proof to accept responsibility to bring on his side the argument for the one case where he claims that the general rule does not hold. The burden of the proof lies not with the pacifist so much as with the advocate of military preparedness. When Barth says that the pacifist has not yet proven the hundredth percent although he is ninety-nine percent right, he himself ought to prove much more clearly his one percent. The pacifist, simply because he is, as Barth admits, in the main line of the will of God in wanting to defend life, is considered narrow and legalistic. But normally it is the person who advocated deviation from the main line of God's will, in the interest of a special case of God's will, who should feel a special obligation to bring the clear reasons for making an exception. For this purpose neither the statement in *CD* III/4 that a people can have a special relationship to God, nor the argument in the wartime writings that the protection of the political structure of a relatively more just state is a duty for Christians, has been founded upon Christian revelation.

Here Barth has permitted himself to remove ethics from the field of dogmatics. What he began by labeling the freedom of God has turned out to be the autonomy of pragmatic political judgment.

We may now hazard a retrospective summary on the systematic ethical problem in Barth's approach. To say that ethics must be derived from the Word of God in the situation is a thesis demanding further specification. Its meaning may be that it links an accent on the uncontrollable sovereignty of God and an existentialistic or intuitionist view of human decision so that there can be no systematic ethic at all. There are strands of this,[3] but they are not basic; otherwise *CD* III/4 and the occasional political writings would have been impossible.

A second possible focus would be to hold that God's speaking to men is related to Christ, the Bible, and Christian tradition in such a way that we can best hear him through a corrected orthodoxy; by understanding Christ more profoundly, reading the Bible more adequately, putting casuistic questions more precisely, and sifting Christian traditions more critically. This is what Barth does everywhere else in his theology, and what he is doing most of the time in his ethics. He lays a solid foundation for it in "The Definiteness of the Divine Decision" (*CD* II/2 661ff.) and sets criteria for it in "The Goodness of the Divine Decision" (*ibid.,* 708 ff., including an extended exposition of Rom. 12–15.). It fits with one of the meanings of the concept of *Grenzfall* (Pyrenees) and with the casuistic discussion of the conditions under which abortion or tyrannicide or war may be possible. Yet he shies away from full commitment to careful casuistry; he does not trust its style nor like the people who work that way. He does not significantly cross-reference in *CD* III/4 to the exegetical sections of II/2.

A third focus is that, after having thought carefully about the background of your problems, you do what seems to make the most sense at the time. You survey casuistic thought but do not become its captive. You have "reasons" for your decision, but that claim cannot be proven and does not release you from the ambiguities of having to choose. This

[3] We have noted the intuitionism above, p. 32, n. 2; p. 48; p. 84, n. 3; the appeal to the inscrutability of God we have noted in the "desert" form of the *Grenzfall* argument and in the accusation that the pacifist denies God's freedom.

mood is pervasive especially in the wartime writings. It may be reinforced by the intuitionist focus noted earlier, but it is less subjective. However, it is belied by the vigor and decisiveness, even to the point of rejecting specified false doctrines, of Barth's participation in the struggles of the German church in 1933 and again in 1958.

A fourth possible focus would be the Free Church thesis that the will of God becomes known in the gathered congregation, when proclamation and the present challenge meet in concrete processes of communication, mutual correction, conviction, and commitment. There would be a basis for such a view in Barth's writings on the church, and examples of it in the *Kirchenkampf* experience. Yet in the ethical writings it is not there.

How then shall we choose? Shall we accuse Barth of fundamental inconsistency, promising a sure word from God and then delivering only a human reasoning? Or can we posit a higher unity of these four strands in "the real Barthian synthesis" which however we cannot prove nor repeat after him? I choose to take as the most reliable key the *movement* in Barth's thought, in which he progressively leaves behind the first and third of the foci named above (intuition and situation) and reinforces the other two (careful theologizing and committed churchmanship). This choice in the evaluation of his ethical assumptions permits our closing suggestions regarding his attitude to pacifism.

We can justifiably trust that if Barth had rethought and remolded his approach to the state, if he had found time to move forward from the social ethics which is founded in creation to that which is founded in reconciliation and redemption, he would also have moved forward from a political ethics which assigns without argument an unchallengeable value to the "just state."

On the level of personal ethics, this forward movement has continued markedly since the time when war was treated in *CD* III/4. The rootage of personal ethics in sanctification, under the rubric of discipleship, moves significantly beyond the ethics of "reverence for life" in the context of creation. Here the form of reasoning is more directly christological, and the substance is still more critical of any use of violence.

In conformity with the New Testament one cannot be pacifist in principle, only practically. But let everyone give heed whether, being called to discipleship, it is either possible for him to avoid, or permissible for him to neglect becoming practically pacifist! [4]

On the level of practical involvement as well, Barth's movement continued in the same direction. The argument of *CD* III/4 was still written in the light of World War II; it made no reference to atomic armament or the cold war. When the rearmament of Germany began, and when the seriousness of the destructive potential of the new weaponry began, Barth again became politically vocal about Germany.[5]

Neither practical involvement nor the fresh statement on personal ethics led to a new theoretical statement on political ethics. The verbal rejection of a "pacifism of principle" is unchanged. Nevertheless these two samples give ground to surmise that if Barth had come to such a new theoretical statement,[6] he would have found reason to reexamine his earlier assumptions about the mandate and value of the state, the survival of which, in the extreme case, he hitherto had held would justify war.[7] The only other alternative would have to be a movement

[4] *KD* IV/2, 622. The English rendering (*CD* IV/2, 550) considerably softens the thrust of this claim. A most helpful interpretation of the significance of "sanctification" as the grounding of ethics is William Hordern's "Sanctification and Politics in the Theology of Karl Barth" (*Chicago Theological Seminary Register,* April 1962, pp. 6 ff.). This appeal to Christ as the exemplary Man was anticipated in *KD* IV/1, 709-10.

[5] See p. 105, n. 3, and see below, pp. 133 ff.

[6] The last "fragment" of *CD IV*/4, published in 1968, deals with sacramental practice. Inasmuch as it strengthens Barth's commitment to the rejection of infant baptism, it fits with the thrust of "Christian Community and Civil Community," thereby supporting implicitly the challenges we have addressed to his earlier theological evaluation of the divine mission of a people with a democratic government. Yet these implications are nowhere on the surface. For the wider social-ethical questions the practical involvement of the late 1950's will have to be the last word.

[7] In 1962 Barth spoke about the room he had left open for war in *KD* III/4: "Of course that was all written in 1951. . . . I cannot yet completely reject it even now. Nevertheless I would say, that it is perhaps not one of the most felicitous passages in the *Kirchliche Dogmatik*. . . . I first spoke 99 percent against war and the military. I hope this impressed you! It has been said to me that this was some of the sharpest of what had ever been said in this direction." He went on in the interview to condemn as "outright mischief" (*heller Unfug*) the use made of his text by some German politicians as proving that just war is still possible. Next he expressed regret that there had been no reference in *KD* III/4 to atomic weapons. "I could have presented the argument that the appearance of automic weapons has so changed the situation that one must say, 'enough now!' . . . The problem of the just war . . . must also be dealt with with a view to its application, and then I would have had to come to it: 'Atomic war cannot be *bellum iustum*' " (*Stimme der Gemeinde*, 1963, pp. 750 ff.). Cf. his still later expressions, pp. 134 and 136.

back to some kind of "common sense" or "natural" buttressing of the state with arguments foreign to the whole structure of his theology.

Our conclusion is therefore that between Barth and an integral Christian pacifism the only differences lie at points where Barth did not finish working out the implications of his originality.[8] Many Christian pacifists in the past have been less politically responsible than Barth. Against their self-righteousness he makes a necessary point. But the fact remains that Barth's best insights cannot but lead to a kind of rejection of war which, though deeper and more differentiated, at once less optimistic and more hopeful than what he has understood under this name, could still not reasonably be called anything other than "Christian Pacifism."

[8] J. M. de Jong, in his analysis of the ethics of creation ("Karl Barth als Ethicus," *Nederlands Theologisch Tijdschrift,* October 1952, pp. 19 ff.) welcomes the rootage of ethics in creation as if it meant a strong emphasis on the generalizability of an "ethic for Everyman." This is an understandable impression when *KD* III/4 remains the last written word on some questions; yet it belies the original design which called for a return to ethics not only under the rubric of Reconciliation (IV, incomplete) but also under Redemption (V, not even begun). Thus the hints we have sought to gather of movement toward a specifically Christian ethic, meant for all men yet not tailored in its demands to what Everyman is ready to do, are still a more valid basis of projection than de Jong's preference for a system reminiscent of the Orders of Creation.

XV

On Trying to Understand Barth: A Critique of Herberg's Interpretation

This theologian, who abjures apologetics and desires nothing but to expound the Word of God, has been compelled by circumstances to propound views on society and the state that make him into one of the most influential social thinkers of our time. (Will Herberg, *Community, State, and Church,* p. 13.)

A small paperback volume has brought together the translations of three of Karl Barth's occasional writings: *"Evangelium und Gesetz," "Rechtfertigung und Recht,"* and *"Christengemeinde und Bürgergemeinde."*[1] Our present interest is in the "Introduction" by the editor, Will Herberg, which makes up over a fourth of the book, under the title "The Social Philosophy of Karl Barth." After our own survey of some of the same materials from Barth's pen, we shall now weigh the adequacy of Herberg's interpretation.

The tone of Herberg's introductory analysis is set by his concern for

[1] Cf. p. 97, n. 2.

the philosophical underpinnings of a social ethic. His center of attention will then be Barth's definition, as it changes, of the rootage and the routing of what the Christian can say to society. The earlier Barth had no social ethics[2]; the later Barth has; then the shift from no to yes is what is most interesting.

It is not made quite clear why in his earlier stages Barth could not offer a basis for a social ethic (in fact Herberg later returns to report that the early "pre-Barthian" Barth was a Christian socialist [p. 22]). Notwithstanding the imprecision of the reporting, let us follow Herberg into his major question: How can the political order be understood theologically?

"In Western thinking, there have been two ways . . ." (p. 24). The "catholic" concepts of natural law or natural order cannot suit Barth because of the assumptions they make about man's goodness and capacity for revelation; but the "augustinian-reformed" vision of necessary compromise or orders of preservation is likewise unacceptable, since it too defines a realm other than redemption, a space in which Christ is not the last and only Word. But where then can he go for a new orientation or foundation? Herberg's answer leaps from the early 1930's, where he posed the question, to 1946 and the publication of "The Christian Community and the Civil Community." The answer here is that the church as community of faith provides a model or analogue, whence guidance can be derived for what the church says to the political community.[3] In rapid succession Herberg says first that this is certainly a strange understanding of the state, then that its strangeness should not make us dismiss it without examination, then that it is ingenious in its thoroughness and consistency, and then that it is hardly convincing. The *method* of analogy is logically not convincing, the *concept* of analogy is more platonic than biblical, and the *substance* of political guidance which Barth supplies is after all the same as what the "augustinian-reformation" concept of the order of preservation would say. The ingenuity is dictated by Barth's effort to claim Christ as the fountainhead

[2] Herberg segregates three early stages in Barth's thought; of all of them it is true (p. 24) that politics is uninteresting. The movement from the third to the fourth then comes in the early 1930's.

[3] Cf. above, p. 100, my treatment of the social ethics of analogy.

of all he says, but it only confuses the structure of what he will actually say.

From here Herberg backtracks to a review of Barth's activity and writing in the 1930's, under the heading "Barth's Encounter with National-Socialism." This highly condensed survey perceives a progression from a theological concern whose political incidence was only derivative, to a point where discriminate political judgments are themselves theologically necessary. At the outset Barth was denying any concern for the Nazi social order as such, but only for those who, explaining as Christians their interest in it, took refuge in it for wrong theological reasons. By 1938 he was affirming an "inward and vital connection" between justification and justice, and was able to move into outspoken partisanship for the allied cause as early as the occupation of Czechoslovakia.

With minor reservations, Herberg commends this movement and the substance of Barth's thought in these years as powerful, profound, balanced, penetrating, sober, passionate, "the thinking of a great Christian theologian who has learned to take politics and culture with the utmost seriousness without for a moment abandoning his ultimate standpoint of faith . . ." (p. 55). But then the wind changes: "Unfortunately, the same cannot be said about Barth's encounter with Communism in the postwar years. It seems an altogether different Barth who is speaking, a Barth who has forgotten everything he had learned and taught the previous fifteen years." The failure of Barth to take toward the Soviet presence and the People's Democratic governments in Eastern Europe the same rigorously negative attitude he took toward Hitler can be described—though even the straight description loses the sensitive selectivity which the 1933-45 digest had had, as Herberg's sense of shock shows through—but it cannot really be understood. "It is perhaps better not to inquire too closely into such matters; it would get nowhere" (p. 63). Thus in a condescending mantle of mock charity the respectful description gives way to school spirit: "Barth's failure to integrate his theology of politics, despite the profundity of his insights, makes the Christian realism of Reinhold Niebuhr particularly relevant." Barth's thought still has some merits at other points, namely those not under discussion in this book, "a depth-understanding of the Christian faith," but the last verdict on the social relevance of that strength is that it correlates with weak political thinking. With this backhanded praise of his depth as a systematician Barth is ushered back out of the field of social thought as at best a deficient Niebuhrian after all.

In the body of this book I have indicated sufficiently that I am aware, as is Herberg, of point-by-point shortcomings which can be discerned in Barth's logic. Critical analysis has not been limited to the social writings of Barth, as is Herberg's, but has gone into their rootage in *Church Dogmatics*. It is then not an uncritical disciple's respect for Barth which is operative when I now turn to the objections which must be addressed to the heavy-handed methods and polemic conclusions of Herberg's description. Herberg's slant shows through clearly only in the last section where Barth's refusal to bless Western anticommunism is evidently the offense; but perhaps that is only the surfacing of a deeper failure to understand.

One of the turnings in Herberg's path is his forsaking of the chronological seriousness with which he had begun. After discerning with some precision four stages in Barth's theological movement, the movement stops with the "late Barth," dated as "1932 to date" (p. 15). The movement stops because Herberg was measuring the movement by only one yardstick: whether Barth has anything to say to social ethics. Before 1919 he did, then until 1932 he could speak only of discontinuity; then begins the "late Barth" who can speak responsibly; from then there is no significant change (when measured by this yardstick) until the regrettable postwar relapse into something which seems (to Herberg) much like the pre-1932 indifference to social ethics. Such a simple yardstick is not wrong or dishonest, but it is hardly adequate when the pattern it makes visible is an erratic zigzag. What matters in interpreting anyone's thought is certainly not only whether he speaks, but also what he says and why he speaks when he does.

It is the oversimplification of the "whether" yardstick, linked to his forsaking in midstream the developmental sequence of analysis, which permits Herberg to leap to the "analogy" theme of the 1946 pamphlet on the two communities, as if it were Barth's only alternative to the dilemma of natural law versus the orders of preservation. Thus he imposes the 1946 concept of analogy as an explanation (p. 43) upon the 1938 text which has a quite different thrust, namely a salvation-history vision of the subjection of the "powers" under Christ's lordship.

If one is to be fair to the story of Barth's social thought, it must be told as a continuing story rather than as an oscillation between "now you have an ethic" and "now you don't," an oscillation for which one cannot find a respectful explanation.

We shall return to an effort to retell this story more fairly; but first we must note at least two of the other points where Herberg's analysis fails to fit his object. One of them is philosophical-theological; it has to do with the meaning of Barth's primary concern for the character of Christian theology. Herberg's one criterion-question is, "Do you have a foundation for social ethics?" yet he does not analyze the implicit theology of his own conception of what constitutes a social ethic. That conception is drawn from common sense, or from Reinhold Niebuhr, or from the history of the labor movement, or from who-knows-where. In any case it is neither defined nor defended before it is drawn in to measure Barth. If Herberg had given some attention to the "depth-perception of the Christian faith given to few in our time" for which he backhandedly gives Barth credit, he would have noticed that his own confident possession of a criterion of what constitutes a social ethic and what does not is itself a normative revelation-claim which would need to be critically explained. For Barth, however difficult the program may be to carry out, every such claim must be critically explained in the light of Christ. Herberg does not tell us how he plans critically to explain his; he just takes it for granted, assuming both its clarity and its relevance. He thus undertakes the reading of Barth with a hermeneutic stance which is structurally antipathetic to Barth's concerns, however respectful he will be in the reading up until 1946. Barth once said (whether we think he brought it off or not) that the only presupposition of a commentary should be that the apostolic author knew what he was saying and that the commentator's job is to interpret his author, not to pass judgment on him. Herberg does not make such an assumption; the longer Barth goes on, the less Herberg can explain it. Herberg takes as a "social philosophy" what for Barth is a segment of Christian theology.

The other major flaw in Herberg's description is his neglect of Barth's participation in the second German church struggle in the late 1950's, when the *Kirchliche Bruderschaften* sought to precipitate a confrontation within the evangelical churches on the issues of rearmament and nuclear weapons. This made it all the more visible that the non-anticommunist position which predominated in the early '50's, though it looked like indifference when measured by Niebuhr's views on Hungary, was a very apt and responsible contribution to the German and Swiss scene, and one in real continuity with the struggle of the '30's.[4] Herberg might have disagreed with Barth, but had he read the *Kirchliche Bruderschaften* story he could not have branded it as a refusal to take sides or as a retreat from the anti-Hitler committedness.

It now remains to us to suggest, as an alternative to Herberg's account, and apart from the pacifist issue which dominates the earlier pages of this book, an empathetic reconstruction of the path of Barth's movement, with regard to Herberg's problem. Let us begin where Herberg does, with the choice between orders of nature and the orders of preservation as social *leitmotifs*. For Herberg these are the two major options, but from where Barth stands they are not to be equally rejected. Natural law, if taken seriously, means a counterrevelation claim; this Barth must reject. But what Herberg calls the "augustinian-reformation view" is not its polar opposite; for it too affirms the priority of an independently knowable creation, of which "preservation" is the defense. But this prior knowledge of creation, when seen as the Reformation saw it, as the locus of the orders of family, state, economy, etc., is just a reworded natural law. Preservation, whose main outlines are traced from the orders of creation, still faintly discernible despite the Fall, is thus the Trojan horse which brought natural theology back into Reformation thought.

The alternative is to reverse the order of gospel and law, as Barth does both in the first essay in the Herberg collection and in his *Church Dogmatics* III. Creation order cannot be affirmed or described apart from Christ; if "preservation" has any place, it is not as the shadow which Creation left behind but as the light which Reconciliation casts before itself.

Then "Justification and Justice" is the normal next step. Borrowing from Schmidt, Dehn, and others the view of Romans 13 which Oscar Cullmann is the strongest advocate today, Barth sees the state as one of the rebellious powers brought into subjection to the lordship of the risen

[4] Just one excerpt from this story is offered in the Appendix, p. 133.

Christ, but not yet totally defeated. This is a new position in contemporary theology in a number of ways:

a. It does not distinguish, as does most political theory of *both* the positions described above, between good states and bad ones, and require obedience to the good ones. It explains why Jesus and Paul practiced and taught subjection to Pilate and Caesar.

b. The attitude to take to the state is then not derived from a reading of its performance, but from the confession of Christ's lordship. That "the powers that be are of God" is not an empirical statement about how well some statesmen are doing; it is a dogmatic statement about the triumph of Christ.

Consequently one cannot use with confidence the concept of the righteous state[5] or the "state properly so-called," so as to disqualify some states as evil. Barth does not, however, pursue this insight to its conclusion in 1938. The rest of his treatise reverts rather to the juxtaposition of Romans 13, with its positive view of the state, and Revelation 13, where the other possibility is dealt with. The end of the essay reaffirms some elements of the augustinian-reformation understanding of the state as divine institution, exemplified in its demands for loyalty and military service, and further justified by its democratic form. Yet the unoriginal character of the last pages of the essay does not justify forgetting the creative promise of its beginnings.[6]

[5] Herberg's texts consistently translate *Rechtsstaat* in ways which contribute to reinforcing a wrong concept. Sometimes it is rendered "legitimate state" and sometimes "just state." For each of these, a different German expression would be used. Each of these fosters the idea of ruling that certain *other* states are *unjust* or *illegitimate,* and the state we approve is somehow positively righteous. This is not what *Rechtsstaat* means (cf. above, p. 50). What is meant is that a state is thought of as recognizing, implementing, and being bound by some thinkable *justice* beyond itself and its arbitrary judgments. The "justice-state" is the modest, self-limiting state. It will still not be just or righteous; but it has set its moral limits. The alternative to *Rechtsstaat* is not "unjust state" or "illegitimate state" but arbitrary authority.

[6] Commentators usually say that Barth has implicitly undermined, if not retracted, this insertion of the state under the "principalities and powers," by his later denial of the real existence of evil angelic beings (see above, p. 97, also John Godsey, ed., *Karl Barth's Table Talk,* pp. 71-72).

Yet the Pauline conception of the "powers" is not dependent upon conceiving them as possessing a particular kind of angelic existence, nor as being unequivocally evil. (Hendrik Berkhof, *Christ and the Powers,* trans. by J. Yoder [Scottdale, Pa.: Herald Press, 1962], pp. 18 ff., disentangles the concepts of "powers" and "angels" quite convincingly.)

We are here concerned with the creative implications of the movement of Barth's thought, not only with what he actually affirms. In this sense we need not consider the

The next innovative step is the distinction between "the Christian Community and the Civil Community" which is the original contribution of the 1946 pamphlet by that name. Herberg reads it as a document on the relationship of two *realms,* faith and ethics; or two disciplines; or two levels of reality. But Barth begins by recognizing that the difference that matters is another one, namely between the People of God and the other peoples. That there could be a distinction between ethics for Christians and ethics for the civil community had not been a constitutive part of Christian social thought since Augustine. One could distinguish clergy and laity, or body and soul, or revelation and reason, or personal and social ethics, or law and gospel, or love and justice—but Barth now distinguishes *communities* and identifies the impossibility of tailoring Christian ethics to fit the civil society.

What is novel about the pamphlet is not the suggested "solution," namely the consistent argument by analogy[7] which is probably proffered tongue-in-cheek anyway,[8] but rather the recognition of the problem it pretends to solve. For Aquinas, Luther, Calvin, Harnack, Brunner, and the Niebuhr brothers, the distinctness of church and world is not an axiom for ethics.[9] Ethical thought is to guide the whole *corpus christianum,* especially the leaders and rulers of society.

The coming to prominence of the concept of *Gemeinde* in Barth's thought is a post-1932 development which Herberg misses by leaping

---

founding of the state in "Justification and Justice" as having been revoked by Barth; it certainly has not been replaced with another complete, systematic answer.

[7] On the strictly logical level, Herberg is of course right that this kind of analogy has no proof value, nor even any sure hermeneutic value; all Barth's commentators agree here; cf. above, pp. 100-102.

[8] Cf. below, p. 128, our reference to Barth's "humor" as it relates to the seriousness of Herberg's critique.

[9] Lutheranism and its pietist offshoots worked out most systematically a duality of ethical realms, emphasizing that the obligations of one's *station* (father, prince, merchant) are the same for the Christian as for the Turk. A duality is maintained between this level of general ethical obligation and the gospel, but what one should *do* in society as faithful Christian, unfaithful Christian, or Turk is the same. The point of the law/gospel duality is to preserve the denial that social-ethical insights or obligations are different for the believing community. Niebuhrian language can speak of a tension between church and world; but it means a difference between worthy and unworthy ethical goals for a whole society, or a conflict between incommensurate leadership structures in a pluralistic society, not the distinction between the community of faith heralding the acts of God on one hand and the givenness of the total social order on the other.

from 1932 to 1946 and back. *Gemeinde* means congregation, rather than "church" in some more hierarchical or structural sense, though it does not mean only a strictly local gathering. It is the gathering-under-the-Word, of which the local assembly is the typical but not the exclusive form. Barth's increasing seriousness about this centering of ethical thought in the really gathered church derives partly from his experiences in the German church struggle, where such a church-against-the-world actually came into being; partly from spelling out the implications of his theology of preaching; partly from continuing concern with what the preaching of the Word of God means to the hearer (cf. his simultaneous movement toward the rejection of infant baptism); partly from his ecumenically appreciative assimilation of some of those strands of pietism which had sowed into European Protestantism the seeds of ecumenical, missionary, and social concern (Zinzendorf, Blumhardt); and partly from continued working with the concept of peoplehood in covenant theology.

Seen thus in terms of its own structure, Barth's thought in the late 1950's about Marxism and about the remilitarization of West Germany is consistent with, not a relapse from, the main lines of his thought over the years.

a. There is what is sometimes called "ultimate indifference"; a label referring not to a lack of interest but to the refusal to accept the state as an object of ultimate concern. We can be free and objective in speaking to or of the state only when we sense the penultimate character of political issues.
b. Within this posture there will be discriminating judgments on socio-political issues. These will not be derived deductively from any one political theory. They may be cloaked in the language of analogy, or even of natural law ("the justice-state") if that helps to communicate.
c. The line between the tolerable state, submission to which includes the renunciation of political subversion, and the persecuting state which forfeits its right to be obeyed, is drawn not by the theologian wielding a criterion of the stateness of the state, but by the state itself when it persecutes the church or Israel.

One of the characteristics of Barth's theological method which it is probably impossible to perceive through translation, or at a distance, or through sober analysis of his writings, is what Barth called "humor." By this he meant not wittiness nor punning nor joke-telling, but a measure of not-taking-oneself-too-seriously. There could be a playful self-spoofing whimsicality about Barth's humor, evident to one who knew him but hard to prove on paper, part of his testimony that for our self-respect we should trust not in our earnestness but in grace. The distinctness of the two communities, the priority of faith over unfaith, and the normative, model-building function of the church in society are quite serious; but after having tried to take the twelve analogies seriously (above, p. 101) it seems to me increasingly likely that in lining them up in apparent formal parallelism, in making them come out with the sacred round number of twelve, Barth was writing with his tongue in his cheek and a try-this-on-for-size twinkle in his eye. Even if only half of the parallels are really parallel, and only a few of the pieces of counsel to society can be tested out, the stance which they illustrate may still be theologically right, and the illustration may still be counted as successful.

Barth does not mean, in any case, that analogy is a reliable, casuistically foolproof process of ethical deliberation. As to *method* in ethical deliberation, Barth stands right where he did before. Partly he will play by ear (what the technicians would call situation or intuition ethics); partly he will center on the warding off of idolatry, not taking the social order too seriously unless it takes itself too seriously. He will use any language and any theological heritage to clothe his points, without becoming committed to the premises of any system. The language of analogy is one quite fitting form in which the social critic can clothe his witness.

Within these assumptions, it may be possible to restate Barth's case against Herberg's criticism:

1. It is not the business of the church to rule on the legitimacy of a state (i.e., by asking how democratic it is) unless the state itself so rules negatively by active persecution. Eastern European Protestants, with whom Barth was in conversation in the '50's (as Herberg does not claim to be), enjoyed at that time as much freedom as they were structurally or theologically ready to use, more than they had ever had before under Austro-Hungarian Catholic or Slavic Orthodox or Turkish Muslim regimes. For these churches to be pro-Western and antisocialist because their government did not meet Western democratic standards (which hardly any government on their side of the

Elbe ever had) would have been to abandon any local social relevance, in the name not of the gospel but of a particular political theory.

2. The gospel is on the side of the poor; not because of Barth's especially weak third analogy (the Son of Man came to seek the lost) but for deeper reasons expressed in what Jesus and the prophets say about mammon and about the orphan. The mystical or prophetic ideal behind Marxism is at this deep level Judeo-Christian, whereas that behind laissez-faire capitalism is enlightenment-humanist. Marxism has a biblical goal but wrong methods; Western individualism provides more tolerable methods (for those who are successful within it) but a wrong goal. In this respect, fascism and Marxism are categorically different, despite the acceptance of totalitarian methods which they may have in common.

3. The Christian's discriminating political judgment will not center on issues of structure. Herberg thinks Marxism and Hitler should be treated just alike because when measured by democratic standards they both stand condemned. Democratic form is then the ultimate yardstick. Barth clearly prefers democracy; he calls it a desirable "expansion" of the Christian unerstanding of the state (cf. Herberg, p. 145). But he cannot make of the presence or absence of democracy the black/white distinction between acceptable and unacceptable orders. Barth is more Pauline in accepting any regime as being under Christ's lordship, and more realistic in knowing that democratic forms are no guarantee of democratic reality (Latin America!).

Herberg's analysis, in summary, saw a progression from indifference to social ethics (1920-30), then toward a serious social philosophy which he could respect (1935-45; in three essays in his book), followed by an inexplicable relapse in the 1950's. I have sought to show step by step the inappropriateness of this analysis; yet if I have succeeded I, too, am left with a problem: namely to explain the wartime writings which Herberg liked best.

From where we now stand in the exposition of Barth's thought, it can be shown by internal analysis that some of the concepts of the wartime period do constitute a deviation from the line which is clear before and after. Setting aside the theme of the Gemeinde/world distinction, which was already developing in his other writings, Barth strikes in the wartime writings the elect-people chords which have had a special resonance in the Swiss psyche since Wilhelm Tell, and in Swiss Protestantism since Zwingli. Forsaking his "ultimate indifference," he identifies the Hitler state as unqualifiedly evil, as no longer under the lordship of Christ,[10] because when measured by the essence of the state it is clearly evil in intention, so that to fight against a particular Nazi operation is to fight for Christ and his church (i.e., defending Czechoslovakia against occupation; cf. Herberg, p. 47). Here it is evident that the natural-law concept of the "essence of the state" is more than the clothing for a situational witness: Here it has become the keystone of the whole argument that Hitler's regime is categorized objectively, factually, not simply as a deficient state or an unjust state but as anti-state (*Unstaat*). The self-evident character of the anti-state status of "more than one other state" (Herberg, p. 143), the clarity with which it may be assumed that a given government is either in or out of this category, are all marks of the natural-law epistemology. The movement from the primary description of the church's duty as *subjection* (Herberg, pp. 134 ff.) to the duty to destroy the anti-state passes by the bridge of the self-defense of separate

[10] "Justification and Justice" assumes, without sensing any need to argue this point, that the state exists in one of two forms; either the demonic-but-usable state of Rom. 13, to which one should be subject, even to the point of combating its enemy states, or the "beast out of the Abyss" of Rev. 13, to which one should not be subject, but which should be destroyed. As logical as this two state theory is to the modern juridical mind, it is not biblical. The duty of Christians in Rev. 13 is *still* to be subject, not to crusade against the beast. The subjection of Rom. 13:1 is still limited and qualified, part of the nonresistant nonconformity of Rom. 13 and 13:8 ff. Cf. J. Yoder, *The Christian Witness to the State* (Newton, Kansas: Faith and Life Press, 1964), p. 76.

A contemporary reflection of the shift in stance represented by the writings of the late 1930's and 1940's is Paul Lehmann's defense of Barth, under the somewhat unlikely title of *Forgiveness: Decisive Issue in Protestant Thought* (New York: Harper & Brothers, 1940). An appendix speaks of the struggle of the Confessing Church in Germany. By Lehmann's criteria not only the Hromádka letter but already "Justification and Justice" represent a backward move away from the genius of Barth's approach:

> "The letter to Dr. Hromádka urges the resistance of the Czech army to German invasion as a battle for Jesus Christ. The monograph on the church and the state undertakes to commit the body of Christ to a virtual crusade against the tyrants in Berlin. This counsel means that Barth is continuing the undialectical tendencies which latterly have crept into his theological thought. . . . The concern for the strictly consequential exposition of the doctrine of the sovereign word of God has been replaced momentarily by the concern for a critical human situation (demonic, to be sure, but nevertheless, human)." (P. 207.)

Lehmann interprets the change in Barth's favor, as a commendable sacrifice of consistency to relevance, while he cites Reinhold Niebuhr as seeing it in the proof that Barth's original view could never handle political issues.

national units[11]; the fact that there can be no questioning of the national unit, or that subjection cannot be attached to any other unit of government, is again assumed, not explained theologically.[12]

It is then the wartime writings, with their unqualified[13] support of one military cause, which represent a detour from the major growth direction of Barth's social thought, not his measured stances of the late '30's. Herberg is right in discerning a difference, but his inattentiveness to the inner structure of Barth's thought, and his own high valuation of democratic anticommunism keep Herberg from seeing which is "the real Karl Barth."

[11] With all the confident vigor with which the non- or anti-state status of Hitler's government was argued by Barth in 1938-45, it is not easy to understand the particular shading of the responses called for. Barth's close friends in German Protestantism largely accepted service in the military and intelligence arms of government; the duty to destroy the non-state or to refuse to be subject to the anti-state as Barth interpreted it was thus not directly incumbent upon the Germans. We noted that even the participation of D. Bonhoeffer in the plot on Hitler's life is not given blanket approval. Other nations, however, especially the bourgeois "Christian" democratic countries of "Czechoslovakia, Holland, Denmark, Scandinavia, France, and, above all, England" faced the duty not only of defending their frontiers but also of defeating Hitler; Switzerland should stay vigilant within a fortified, pro-Allied neutrality. There is some discussion of the special mission of Swiss neutrality, but I do not remember finding any discussion of why the duty of the allied democracies to destroy Nazism was not linked with a duty of the Christians in Germany to be disloyal.

[12] If we were seeking a fuller catalog of the "non-Barthian" strains in the wartime writings, another would be a very evident "pastoral" (others would call it "religious") concern for the morale of the Swiss nation. That the business of the church is to help people in general feel confident and manly is a theme not usually associated with Barth's approach to either preaching or theology, but there are traces of it in wartime writings.

[13] The term "unqualified" needs qualification. Barth continues to say that the war is not "identified with the church's cause," but the church should consecrate this cause as Christ's (Herberg, p. 53) and no longer see it as morally abhorrent (*ibid.*, p. 52 and p. 54, n. 125; above p. 41, n. 1; p. 49, n. 1).

APPENDIX:
The Continuing Church Struggle

When in the 1950's the curtain dividing Germany continued to harden and the formation of a Federal Republic in the West enabled Germans to become part of the North Atlantic defense system, those German Protestants who had formerly been together in the Confessing Church's opposition to Hitler found themselves divided. Some, among them Hans Asmussen, Helmut Thielicke, and Eberhard Müller, supported the Christian Democratic party and government of Chancellor Konrad Adenauer, including Adenauer's readiness to rearm. Others, represented by Martin Niemöller and with Barth's sympathy, were convinced that Christians should again be in the opposition. Informal groups called "church brotherhoods" (*Kirchliche Bruderschaften*), claiming the heritage and some of the membership of the Confessing Church, became the bearers of this protest, and addressed it with increasing sharpness to the particular issue of *atomic* armament.

The high point of this wave of protest, and a fitting final document in our report of Karl Barth's own continuing commitment, was a petition (*Anfrage*) addressed by the *Bruderschaften* in March, 1958, to the Synod of the Evangelical Church in Germany (the federative body then grouping most of the Protestants of both Germanies). The core of this text was a series of ten articles, which are here reproduced with their immediate context:

I. The Evangelical Church confesses that in Jesus Christ she finds "joyous liberation from the Godless bonds of the world unto free, thankful service to His creatures." (Barmen Thesis 2.) This forbids to her not only any approval of or collaboration in an atomic war and its preparation, but also her tacitly letting it happen. This awareness demands that in the obedience of faith . . . here as in every issue . . . we ourselves must take the first step to hold back the threatening destruction and to trust more in the reality of the Word of God than in the "realism" of political calculation. The first step is the act of *diakonia* which we, as Christians, owe to the menaced and anxious world of today. Let the faithless hesitate . . . ; we as Christians may and must dare it in trust in God, who created this World and every living creature in East and West for the sake of the suffering and victorious Jesus Christ, and will preserve the same through Christ and the preaching of His Gospel until His Day.

II. If the Synod finds itself unable to assent to this confession, we must ask how the Synod can refute it on the grounds of Scripture, the Confessions, and reason.

For the sake of the men and women for whom we are responsible, and for our own sakes, we must insist upon receiving an answer to this question. We owe it to the Synod to remind it of its spiritual responsibility, since it is in the shouldering of this responsibility that it shows itself to be the legitimate authority in the Church. It is our conviction that in the face of this issue the Church finds herself in the *status confessionis*.[1]

[1] Much of the debate about the Ten Articles centered on the meaning of this phrase. *Status confessionis* designates that situation in which the church is challenged to take sides, with her very existence as church being at stake. The later debate had to do with the sense in which the choice of this phrase meant a personal condemnation of anyone holding another view. Cf. article 10 below.

If the Synod agrees with us, that an unreserved *No* is demanded of Christians facing the problem of the new weapons, must she not also say promptly and clearly to the State, that the true proclamation of the Gospel, also in the Chaplaincy, includes the testimony that the Christian may not and cannot participate in the design, testing, manufacture, stocking and use of atomic weapons, nor in training with these weapons?

III. We, therefore, ask the Synod whether she can affirm together with us the following ten propositions, for the instruction of consciences concerning Christian behavior with regard to atomic weapons:

1. War is the ultimate means, but always, in every form a questionable means, of resolving political tensions between nations.
2. For various reasons, good and less good, churches in all lands and all ages have hitherto not considered the preparation and the application of this ultimate means to be impossible.
3. The prospect of a future war to be waged with the use of modern means of annihilation has created a new situation, in the face of which the Church *cannot* remain *neutral.*
4. War, in the form of *atomic war,* means the mutual annihilation of the participating peoples as well as of countless human beings of other peoples, which are not involved in the combat between the two adversaries.
5. War, in the form of atomic war, is therefore seen to be *an instrument incapable of being used* for the resolution of political conflicts, because it destroys every presupposition of political resolution.
6. Therefore, the Church and the individual Christian can say nothing but an *a priori No* to a war with atomic weapons.
7. Even preparation for such a war is under all circumstances *sin against God and the neighbor,* for which no Church and no Christian can accept responsibility.
8. We therefore demand in the Name of the Gospel that an *immediate end be made* to preparations for such a war within our land and nation regardless of all other considerations.

9. We challenge all those who seriously want to be Christians to *renounce,* without reserve and under all circumstances, any participation in preparations for atomic war.
10. In the face of this question, the opposing point of view, or neutrality, *cannot be advocated* Christianly. Both mean the denial of all three articles of the Christian faith.[2]

As of early March 1958, this text had 364 signatures, largely from among the Protestant clergy of West Germany, gathered in nine provincial *Bruderschaften.* The submission and publication of this text set loose a flood of debates, expositions, declarations, and counterdeclarations in the church and secular press. A further meeting of the *Bruderschaften* was called in Frankfurt for that fall, to which Karl Barth was invited. A portion of the letter in which he stated his inability to attend follows; its words form a fitting conclusion to our study:

> . . . It is perhaps also good if I am not there in person—among other reasons because the younger generation must learn to push more and more into the front lines and to fight the battles which must be waged on the practical-theological front, on the basis of their own insight and responsibility . . . . This, however, does not mean that I in any way withdraw from my preoccupation with the problems to be dealt with in Frankfurt. These problems have also become significant here in Switzerland in a very special way, and demand my daily attention.[3] The West-German *Bruderschaften,* having their origin in, and belonging together with, what happened 25 years ago, should be assured that I am with them wholeheartedly and stand behind them, always, but especially in the concern which disturbs them now, and that I shall continue to do so in the future all the more joyously, the more they continue the pathway upon which they have entered, free of all pro-

[2] Quoted from *Junge Kirche,* March 10, 1958. An earlier draft reportedly included here the sharper phrasing, "and excludes one from the communion of the Church Universal."

[3] Letter in *Junge Kirche,* October 10, 1958. Karl Barth was at this time member of the Theological Commission of the Swiss Evangelical Church Federation, to which the question of atomic armament for the Swiss armed forces was referred. Barth, Jacques Courvoisier, and two others responded with an eight-point statement substantially like that of the *Bruderschaften;* Ernst Staehelin, Eduard Schweizer, and four others denied to the church the authority to settle such technical military matters. The Swiss Reformed Association of Pastors, following a debate at its meeting November 10, 1958, turned down by mail poll a resolution calling on the Swiss military authorities to renounce atomic arms (*Junge Kirche,* January 10, 1959, pp. 52-53).

fundity and despair, clear and decided, uncompromisingly and consistently. What was the rumor spread about in Germany's newspapers, "that Professor Barth is not theologically in agreement with the Ten Theses of the Petition"? You may say to all and to everyone, that I am in agreement with these Theses (including the 10th!), as if I had written them myself,[4] and that I desire nothing more earnestly than that they should be maintained and interpreted worthily, convincingly, and joyfully, but in principle unbendingly, in Frankfurt and thereafter in all the Evangelical Church in Germany.

Whether the Frankfurt meeting will be a "success" [*Erfolg*] is a secondary question beside what I wish you all: namely, that it be dominated and determined by a good spirit of "discipleship [*Nachfolge*]!"

[4] A usually reliable source reported that Barth actually did have a hand in the original draft of the Ten Articles.

Index of Scripture References

Index of Names

Index of Subjects